DORNIER Do 17

IN THE BATTLE OF BRITAIN

DORNIER Do 17
IN THE BATTLE OF BRITAIN

The 'Flying Pencil' in the Spitfire Summer

Chris Goss

AIR WORLD

AIR WORLD

DORNIER Do 17 IN THE BATTLE OF BRITAIN
The 'Flying Pencil' in the Spitfire Summer

First published in Great Britain in 2022 by
Air World
An imprint of
Pen & Sword Books Ltd
Yorkshire – Philadelphia

ISBN 978 1 52678 120 8

A CIP catalogue record for this book is available from the British Library.

Typeset by SJmagic DESIGN SERVICES, India.

Printed and bound in the UK by CPI Group (UK) Ltd.

Pen & Sword Books Limited incorporates the imprints of Atlas, Archaeology, Aviation, Discovery, Family History, Fiction, History, Maritime, Military, Military Classics, Politics, Select, Transport, True Crime, Air World, Frontline Publishing, Leo Cooper, Remember When, Seaforth Publishing, The Praetorian Press, Wharncliffe Local History, Wharncliffe Transport, Wharncliffe True Crime and White Owl.

For a complete list of Pen & Sword titles please contact

PEN & SWORD BOOKS LIMITED
47 Church Street, Barnsley, South Yorkshire, S70 2AS, England
E-mail: enquiries@pen-and-sword.co.uk
Website: www.pen-and-sword.co.uk

Or
PEN AND SWORD BOOKS
1950 Lawrence Rd, Havertown, PA 19083, USA
E-mail: Uspen-and-sword@casematepublishers.com
Website: www.penandswordbooks.com

FSC
www.fsc.org

MIX
Paper | Supporting
responsible forestry
FSC® C013604

Contents

Introduction

As early as March 1933, the Reichswehrministerium (later the Reichsluftfahrtministerium, or RLM) wrote to Dornier Werke GmbH expressing the wish for a 'cargo plane with special equipment' – in other words a bomber. As a result, between 1933 and 1937 Dornier developed and built twenty-one prototypes for various purposes under contract to the RLM.

In October 1935, Dornier revealed its Do 17V1, a twin-engine commercial transport aircraft which had first flown on 23 November 1934. This aircraft would be capable of carrying six passengers at relatively high speed. The Do 17's aerodynamic design together with the twin liquid-cooled BMW VI engines, the most powerful aero engines available in Germany at that time, met this requirement, but also enabled it to achieve speeds nearly 60 mph superior to other aircraft entering service with the embryonic Luftwaffe.

The first units to convert to the Do 17E-1 were I./Kampfgeschwader 153 (I./KG 153) and I./KG 155. Soon after Aufklärungsgruppe (Fern) 122 ((F/122) began converting to the Do 17F-1. The remaining Gruppen of KG 153 and KG 155 converted throughout 1937, with KG 255 forming in the spring of 1937. With this rapid expansion of Do 17-equipped units came the opportunity to test the aircraft in combat, when, in March 1937, the first of three Do 17Es arrived in Spain.

It is thought that the Do 17 flew its first mission on 12 March 1937. Valuable lessons were learnt by the Luftwaffe's Legion Condor – experiences that would prove invaluable some two years later.

With the attack on Poland on 1 September 1939, the campaign saw the largest ever concentration of Do 17s with around 20 Staffeln of Do 17Ps being used for reconnaissance and KG 2, KG 3, KG 76 and KG 77 being used for bomber operations with Do 17E, M and Z in support of ground troops. In addition, nine Stuka Gruppen used small numbers of Do 17M/Ps for support and reconnaissance work.

The first Do 17 operational mission of the Second World War was flown by III./KG 3 against approaches to the railway bridge at Dirschau (now Tczew in Poland). Do 17 losses throughout the campaign were light due to the Luftwaffe's air superiority. However, the Do 17's Achilles Heel still remained its small bomb load and limited range, thus it increasingly became side-lined by the He 111's bigger bomb load and the Ju 88's better speed and range. As a result, even by the end of 1939, production of the Do 17 was already slowing down.

From the start of the war, Do 17s were quite active carrying out reconnaissance missions over France, Belgium and Holland. The first loss on these operations was a Do 17P which suffered engine failure during a reconnaissance of the East Coast of England on 26 October 1939; it force-landed in neutral Holland where its crew were interned. The first Do 17P to be shot down in combat in the West occurred on 30 October 1939, when Pilot Officer Peter 'Boy' Mould of No.1 Squadron shot down an aircraft of 2.(F)/123. It crashed and exploded at Traveron with the death of its crew.

The severe weather of winter 1939-1940 curtailed air operations and it was not until 11 January 1940 that the next Do 17P, from 3.(F)/11, was shot down by the French Groupe de Chasse (GC) I/5. Two days later saw a rare loss when one of just three Do 17S-0s built and operated by 1.(F)/Aufklärungsgruppe Oberbefehlshaber der Luftwaffe was shot down during a high-altitude reconnaissance sortie over southern Britain by GC I/4 and crash-landed near Calais, its crew being captured.

Just one more Do 17M, from 2.(H)/13, was lost in January 1940. February 1940 saw no Do 17 combat losses and it was not until 2 March 1940, that the next losses occurred. Of interest on 31 March 1940, Wekusta 26 lost its first Do 17Z-2 in combat when a Spitfire of 54 Squadron damaged its starboard engine off the Suffolk coast while on a weather reconnaissance sortie. It later crashed in the sea off Ameland with the deaths of all four crew.

By the start of April 1940, the German invasion of France and the Low Countries was now just forty days away and with an improvement in the weather, air operations began to increase. A total of four Do 17s were shot down in combat and another four damaged during the month, but by now a number of Do 17 units had begun to convert to the Ju 88.

Further north, on 8 April 1940, German forces invaded Norway. However, the part played by the Do 17 was minimal due to the ranges the aircraft would have to fly. The only Do 17 unit to take an active part, 1.(F)/120, only had five Do 17Ps and three He 111s, and shortly after the campaign began to hand over the former in favour of the He 111. Küstenfliegergruppe 606 also carried out coastal armed reconnaissance in the seas between Germany and Norway with one Do 17Z-3 failing to return from a mission on 9 April 1940. Because of its maritime nature, Küstenfliegergruppe 606 would later operate the Do 17Z-5, a Z-3 equipped with additional floatation and survival equipment, notably two flotation devices which were fixed either side of the nose.

Meanwhile further south, the first nine days of May 1940 were relatively quiet. The last reported combat was between a Do 17P of 4.(F)/121 intercepted by 87 Squadron on 9 May 1940, which managed to return with a wounded crew member.

On 10 May 1940, the Battle of France began. KG 2, KG 3, KG 76 and KG 77 were all in action and all suffered casualties; indeed, the loss of 23 Do 17s on the first day of the campaign was not good.

Over the days and weeks that followed, the Do 17 remained in action over Western Europe. Towards the end of May and into June, the scene of battle started switching to the Channel coast and, in particular, Dunkirk.

The Do 17 first made an appearance en masse in British airspace on 3 July 1940. By now, the only Do 17 bomber units were KG 2 and KG 3 – II./KG 76 was converting to the Ju 88 and KG 77 was about to start the same process. It was, therefore, a bitter pill for KG 77 that on 3 July 1940, 1./KG 77 would lose an aircraft, as would 2./KG 77, 8./KG 77 and 9./KG 77. In addition, Stab/KG 2 suffered an aircraft very badly damaged and another from 3./KG 3 came down in the Channel. All were as a result of fighter action and only one came down on land.

There would now be a series of convoy attacks in the days leading up to 10 July 1940, the official start of the Battle of Britain. The only casualties were two aircraft from II./KG 2 damaged in combat on 4 July 1940, and another from III Gruppe damaged on 7 July 1940. Everything, however, was about to change.

Glossary

Crew roles

1. Wart	Leading Ground Mechanic / Maintenance Man
Beobachter	Observer
Bombenschütze	Bombardier
Bordfunker	Radio Operator
Bordmechaniker	Flight Engineer
Bordschütze	Air Gunner
Feinmech.	Precision Mechanic
Flugzeugführer	Pilot
Flzg.-Mech.	Aircraft Mechanic
Hilfsbeobachter	Auxiliary/Assistant Observer
Kr.Ber.	War Reporter
Prüfer	Technical Examiner
Waffenwart	Armourer-Artificer

Ranks

Feldwebel	Flight Sergeant
Flieger	Aircraftman
Gefreiter	Leading Aircraftman
Hauptmann	Flight Lieutenant/Captain
Leutnant	Pilot Officer/Second Lieutenant
Major	Squadron Leader/Major
Oberfeldwebel	Warrant Officer
Obergefreiter	Senior Aircraftman/Corporal
Oberleutnant	Flying Officer/First Lieutenant
Oberst	Group Captain/Colonel
Oberstleutnant	Wing Commander/Lieutenant Colonel
Stabsfeldwebel	Senior Warrant Officer
Unteroffizier	Sergeant

General terms

DORNIER Do 17 IN THE BATTLE OF BRITAIN

Deutsches Kreuz in Gold	German Cross in Gold award
Ehrenpokal	Goblet of Honour – awarded for outstanding achievements in the air war
Geschwader	Group consisting of three Gruppen commanded by a Geschwader Kommodore
Gruppe	Wing consisting of three Staffeln; commanded by a Gruppen Kommodore. The Gruppe number is denoted by Roman numerals
Kampfgeschwader	Bomber Group
Kette	Three aircraft tactical formation similar to RAF 'vic'
Ritterkreuz	Knight's Cross
Ritterkreuz mit Eichenlaub	Knight's Cross with Oak Leaves
Stab	Staff or HQ formation in which Gruppen Kommandeur and Geschwader Kommodore flew
Staffel	Squadron (twelve aircraft); commanded by a Staffelkapitän. The Staffel number is denoted by Arabic numerals
Werknummer (W.Nr.)	Serial Number

Chapter 1

July 1940

Although the Battle of Britain did not officially start until 10 July 1940, the Do 17 first made an appearance in British airspace in any great numbers on the third day of the month. By then, the only pure Do 17 bomber units were KG 2, KG 3, and KG 77, as well as I and III./KG 76.

By this stage, II./KG 76 was converting to the Junkers Ju 88 and would be followed by KG 77 later in the month. On what would be their last day of operations with the Do 17 on 3 July 1940, 1, 2, 8 and 9./KG 77 would each lose an aircraft.

There would now be a series of convoy attacks by KG 2 and KG 3 in the days leading up to the start of the Battle of Britain, during which time Do 17 casualties were light. As well as bombing missions, reconnaissance flights were still being flown, but many of the units involved were also converting from the Do 17 to the Ju 88.

It is believed that the first Do 17 casualty of the Battle of Britain, which occurred on the opening day, 10 July 1940, was a Do 17P-1 from 4.(F)/121. This aircraft was badly damaged by Hurricanes of 145 Squadron during a reconnaissance sortie over the area Oxford-Portsmouth-Isle of Wight-Swindon. This was followed later the same day by a Do 17Z of 4./KG 3 which was shot down off the Norfolk coast by Spitfires from 66 Squadron based at RAF Coltishall.

That afternoon, Do 17s of I./KG 2 and III./KG 2 attacked a convoy south of Dover. The crews involved optimistically claimed to have sunk three freighters, when in fact just one of 466 tons was lost. However, three Do 17s were destroyed and a number damaged.

Because of the weather, Do 17 operations the following day appear to have been limited to coastal reconnaissance, but a Do 17 of 4./KG 2 returned with 220 bullet holes, having shot down the 85 Squadron Hurricane responsible. There would be two more losses that day – a Do 17P-1 of 2.(F)/11 which was shot down over the Channel by 601 Squadron and a weather reconnaissance aircraft of Wekusta 26 which was reported missing off the English coast. In addition, an aircraft of 1./KG 3 was also damaged by Nos. 66 and 242 Squadrons.

The scene having apparently been set for the Battle of Britain, the remainder of July 1940 was surprisingly much quieter for the Do 17 units. Bombers carried out armed reconnaissance sorties and the occasional convoy attack, but losses were light. There were, however, a number of casualties from other units, these occurring from as far north as Aberdeen to as far west as Dorset.

Of note is the fact that a small number of Do 17s flying pre- and post-attack reconnaissance missions for Junkers Ju 87 Stuka units were lost over the Channel. At the same time, limited night operations were starting to be flown. However, if July 1940 finished quietly, August 1940 would, after a quiet start, soon see Do 17 operations increase dramatically.

Left: Hauptmann Werner Leuchtenberg's Do 17Z, coded 3Z+DK, of 2./KG 77. KG 77's time over the UK with this type lasted no more than three weeks.

Below: A view of KG 77's unique Eagle badge which had its origins in the Middle Ages. The colours varied depending on which Gruppe an aircraft was operated by.

Right: A hangar full of Do 17s of III./KG 77. The nearest is marked 3Z+FT of Hauptmann Jakob Neuen's 9./KG 77.

Below: The remains of Unteroffizier Richard Brandes' Do 17Z, Werk Nummer (W.Nr.) 2642 and coded 3Z+GS, after it crashed at Paddock Wood on 3 July 1940.

Left: Another view of the wreckage of Unteroffizier Brandes' Do 17 at Paddock Wood. This aircraft had been engaged by three Hurricanes at 8,000ft over Tonbridge. The attacks forced Brandes' crew to jettison its remaining bomb load; they had previously dropped six 50kg on RAF Kenley.

It would seem that Brandes' aircraft provided quite a spectacle for RAF personnel and members of the public alike. Considering the extensive damage, it is remarkable that two of the crew, Brandes and Oberleutnant Hans-Georg Gallion, survived, albeit both were wounded, the latter badly so.

Right: The Do 17 of 6./KG 2's Oberfeldwebel Hans Wolff, seen here, was damaged in combat with 79 Squadron on 4 July 1940.

Below: An air-to-air shot of two Do 17 Ps of 3.(F)/123 sporting different camouflage schemes in the summer of 1940.

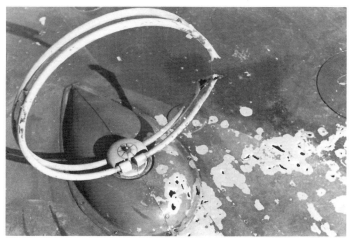

Four images showing combat damage to a Do 17 of 3.(F)/123 that were taken after the aircraft had managed to return to its base in France. It is possible this aircraft was damaged in combat on 10 July 1940. For some reason, it is listed as a 4.(F)/121 aircraft in the Luftwaffe records.

Damaged in combat over the Channel on 10 July 1940, this Do 17Z of 1./KG 2, with the code letters U5+AH, crash-landed near Wimereux.

JULY 1940

Above: A second view of the wreckage of U5+AH after it came down near Wimereux on the opening day of the Battle of Britain. Of the crew, Obergefreiter Georg Kröhl (Flugzeugführer) and Gefreiter Martin Assum (Bordfunker) were wounded, while Feldwebel Franz Enderle (Bordmechaniker) was killed. The fourth member, the Beobachter, Oberfeldwebel Karl Deckarm, was uninjured.

Right: Another casualty on the first day of the Battle of Britain was this aircraft from 2./KG 2, pictured here under guard and having been hastily camouflaged after it crash-landed back in France. Two of the Do 17's crew, Leutnant Heinz Ermecke (Flugzeugführer) and Unteroffizier Götz-Dieter Wolf, can be seen studying their 'plane. They were fortunate to have survived the incident, for their Beobachter, Feldwebel Rudolf Schmidt, had been killed. Ermecke and Wolf would be shot down again on 21 August 1940, at which point the former was killed, the latter captured.

Left: A photograph of a Do 17 approaching the recently occupied Channel Islands during the summer of 1940. Although the codes cannot be discerned, the band around the fuselage would indicate the unit as being KG 76.

Above: Early on the morning of 11 July 1940, Do 17Z W.Nr. 2542, and coded U5+GM, of 4./ KG 2 was intercepted off Harwich by a 85 Squadron Hurricane flown by Squadron Leader Peter Townsend. In the ensuing combat, the Hurricane was shot down, though Townsend was rescued. The Do 17 managed to limp back across the Channel to crash-land at Mory. The Flugzeugführer, Oberleutnant Joachim Genzow was unwounded, while the rest of the crew, Leutnant Walter Bornschein (Beobachter), Oberfeldwebel Werner Borner (Bordfunker) and Feldwebel Friedrich Lohrer (Bordmechaniker) were all wounded. The crew were all decorated later in the war; Genzow and Bornschein were both awarded the Ritterkreuz, while Borner and Lohrer received the Deutsches Kreuz in Gold. Bornschein was killed in action on 27 April 1944.

Above and right: RAF pilots frequently confused the Do 17 with the Do 215 – and these two images show why. The Do 17 is the picture above. In very simple terms, the Do 215 was an export version of the Do 17 with different engines.

Groundcrew pictured working on a Do 17Z of 1./KG 76. The devil emblem below the cockpit is red in colour. Interestingly, the 'Red Devil' has a pistol drawn and a bomb falling from its rear end.

An award ceremony being held for aircrew of an unidentified reconnaissance unit. In the background is a Do 17P.

Above: This Do 17Z is from Stabstaffel/StG 3; one of StG 3's Stukas can be seen in the background. It is known that Stab./StG 3 had at least two Do 17Zs on its strength in October 1940, their W.Nrs. being 2832 and 2877.

Right: A mechanic poses for the camera from the cockpit of an unarmed Do 17Z of an unidentified unit in the summer of 1940.

Recorded as being a Do 17M, as opposed to a P variant, this 4.(F)/14 aircraft, coded 5F+OM, was shot down by Squadron Leader Harold Fenton, Flight Lieutenant Don Turner, Pilot Officer John Wigglesworth and Pilot Officer Charles Davis, all of 238 Squadron, on 21 July 1940. It crashed at Nutford Farm, Blandford in Dorset, at 14.45 hours.

Soldiers examine the still-smouldering wreckage of 5F+OM at Nutford Farm, Blandford, on 21 July 1940.

A member of 5F+OM's crew, lying on a stretcher, is given medical treatment following the crash on 21 July 1940. Leutnant Georg Thiel (Beobachter), Feldwebel Fritz Bohnen (Flugzeugführer) and Unteroffizier Alfred Werner (Bordfunker) were all captured wounded. (Courtesy of Andy Saunders)

This Do 17P of 2.(F)/123, coded 4U+HK, is pictured taxying out at Cherbourg in the summer of 1940.

Above: A photograph of a group of officers of 3.(F)/33. From left to right are Hauptmann Johannes Sieckenius (Staffelkapitän), Oberleutnant Karl Braasch (killed on 15 August 1940), Oberleutnant Hermann Schmidt (with his back to the camera, injured in an accident on 24 November 1940); Leutnant Alexander von Brixen (killed on 28 November 1940) and Leutnant Walter Burmeister (also killed on 28 November 1940).

Left: The Do 17Z coded U5+IH of Oberleutnant Karl Kessel's 1./KG 2 overflying the airfield at Épinoy, again in the summer of 1940.

Above: This is believed to be Hauptmann Reinhard Liebe-Piderit who, as Staffelkapitän of 3.(F)/123, is seen here in front of a Do 17P. An experienced pilot who saw service in Spain, Liebe-Piderit then led his Staffel successfully in Poland and during the Battle of France. He was killed when a French aircraft he was flying crashed at Buc on 19 July 1940. Gefreiter Edmund Thiel was also injured in the accident.

Right: A view of the 'caveman' emblem that was thought to have been used by IV.(Erg.)/KG 3, but which is also said to have been used by I./KG 3. The 'caveman' carries a bomb under his left arm and a trident in his right hand. The background shield was apparently blue.

Left: Another Do 17 with the same 'caveman' emblem on its nose. This badge, or a similar one, was noted on the wreckage of a Do 17Z-2 of 1/KG 3, W.Nr. 2544 and coded 5K+CH, which crashed at Boughton Malherbe in Kent on 28 October 1940. This raider was almost certainly the victim of anti-aircraft fire.

Below: A Do 17Z of I./KG 3 in its improvised pen in the summer of 1940. Note, once again, the same 'caveman' badge seen in a previous image.

A group of Do 17Zs of 9./KG 3. The aircraft nearest to the photographer is that coded 5K+DT.

The wreckage of Dornier Do 17M coded A5+EA, of Stab/StG 1, lies in a field at East Fleet Farm, near Fleet in Dorset, after being shot down at 11.15 hours on 25 July 1940. Undertaking a reconnaissance flight at the time, this aircraft was brought down by a Spitfire of 152 Squadron.

A good shot of a Do 17Z showing the jacking points under the wings.

All that is left of Do 17Z F1+AK of 2./KG 76. This crashed while taking-off at Noalles, France, at 15.30 hours on 30 July 1940.

Right: The crew of F1+AK were all killed in the crash seen in the previous picture. This is the grave marker placed on the spot where Unteroffizier Hans Schmid (Flugzeugführer), Obergefreiter Rudolf von Kaler (Beobachter), Feldwebel Adolf Diesner (Bordfunker) and Unteroffizier Josef Punger (Bordmechaniker) were all initially buried.

Below: A Do 17Z of 9./KG 76 pictured during a low-level training flight off the French coast.

A Do 17 Z of Stab/KG 3; the next bomb load is in the foreground.

Another Do 17Z of KG 3 in its hangar during the summer of 1940.

A Do 17Z-5 of Küstenfliegergruppe 606 photographed at Brest in the summer of 1940. Note the unit badge on the forward fuselage and the floatation aids either side of the nose. This unit converted to the Ju 88 in early 1941 and, in the process, handed many of its aircraft over to KG 2.

This photograph of a Do 17Z-5 of Küstenfliegergruppe 606 clearly illustrates the floatation bulges on the nose.

A Do 17P, coded S2+KA, of Stab./StG 77. This unit used a mixture of Do 17Ms and Ps.

An unidentified Do 17Z of 4./KG 76 pictured having suffered a catastrophic accident of some description. At the end of the Battle of France, II./KG 76 began converting to the Ju 88 and its aircraft were reassigned, retaining the same badges, to I and III./KG 76.

Chapter 2

August 1940

Dornier 17 combat losses for the first ten days of August 1940 were limited to a Do 17P of 4.(F)/14 which was reported missing over the English Channel on 3 August and a Do 17Z of 7./KG 3 which was shot down by 85 Squadron three days later.

Events on 12 August 1940 saw a number of Do 17s carrying out nuisance and decoy flights over south-eastern England, following which I./KG 2 attacked RAF Lympne and then RAF Manston. Early that evening, it was the turn of the whole of KG 2 to target airfields near Canterbury and Dover. Three aircraft from KG 2 returned damaged and with wounded crew.

The Luftwaffe had intended that the following day would be Adlertag or 'Eagle Day'. This was the first day of *Unternehmen Adlerangriff*, which was the codename of the Luftwaffe's plan to destroy the RAF. The weather, however, decreed otherwise, and the poor conditions resulted in many of the attacks failing to materialise.

For some aircraft that were already airborne, efforts were made to recall them. Tasked with bombing RAF Eastchurch, not all of the I./KG 2 crews heard the recall with the result that the remaining aircraft flew on. RAF fighters claimed to have shot down sixteen Do 17s, probably shot down another four and damaged eight. In reality, five were shot down and another seven returned suffering varying degrees of damage.

Two days later, all three Do 17 bomber Geschwader were in action. Mid-afternoon, all of KG 2, together with I and II./KG 3, attacked airfields near the Thames Estuary. KG 2 returned unscathed, but KG 3 suffered a number of casualties. One of Stab I./KG 3 force-landed in France with two crew wounded and another from 2./KG 3 returned with slight damage, but with its pilot mortally wounded. The other losses came from 6./KG 3, which lost two aircraft and another four damaged.

The final raid of the day was undertaken by I and III./KG 76. Targeting the Fighter Command airfields at Redhill and Biggin Hill, this was their first major attack of the Battle of Britain.

On 16 August, the first attack of the day by KG 76 was cancelled. Then an aircraft of Stab III./KG 76 was lost carrying out a high-level attack on RAF West Malling when it collided with a Hurricane of 111 Squadron. At the same time, around twenty-five aircraft from KG 3 headed for Tilbury Docks, but released their bombs before the target.

Two days later, on 18 August 1940, the crews of KG 76 carried out a spectacular low-level attack on RAF Kenley – but not without cost. It was III./KG 76, and in particular 9 Staffel, that suffered badly. An aircraft of 8 Staffel came down in the Channel and in 9 Staffel two aircraft, including that of the Staffelkapitän, came down on British soil, while another two came down in the Channel. The remainder returned with varying degrees of damage.

With poor weather, the next two days were quieter with KG 2 reporting to have carried out a series of armed coastal reconnaissance missions or airfield attacks by single aircraft. If the traditional Do 17 units were waging war over the south-east of England, at the same time maritime bombing unit Küstenfliegergruppe 606 was carrying out daylight armed maritime reconnaissance and precision night attacks against land targets in the west.

From now on night attacks by Do 17s began to feature more and more. Indeed, major daylight attacks would end the following month, but not before a total of sixty-six Do 17s were destroyed on operations.

Another day of poor weather followed on 21 August 1940, though both KG 2 and KG 3 were able to carry out a series of nuisance attacks. Even then, six Do 17s would be lost. The next four days would be quieter with just three Do 17s lost in combat.

With an improvement in the weather, a series of major attacks against British airfields was made on 26 August 1940. Just before midday, a small number of aircraft from 7./KG 3 carried out a diversionary attack against RAF Manston. In the battles that followed, three Do 17Zs crashed into the sea, one was written off crash-landing in France and one more damaged. About two hours later, I./KG 2 took off to attack RAF Hornchurch and III./KG 2 RAF Debden. I Gruppe lost two and III Gruppe suffered three aircraft lost over England.

For the remaining five days of August 1940, KG 2 seems to have concentrated on night attacks with Hull, Harwich, Colchester, Derby and Thameshaven being selected as targets. Surviving Küstenfliegergruppe 606 records show that its focus of effort was now on night operations with few daylight maritime operations. On the nights between 26 and 31 August, they attacked such targets as RAF St Eval, Bristol, Avonmouth, Liverpool/Birkenhead and Falmouth.

The first Do 17 reconnaissance losses for twelve days occurred on 27 August 1940, when 238 Squadron shot down a Do 17P of 3.(F)/31 over Devon, and then 56 and 501 Squadrons shot down another from 3.(F)/10 off Cap Gris Nez. There would be one more loss, a Do 17P of 3.(F)/22, over the North Sea on 30 August 1940. This was the last Do 17 reconnaissance loss until 5 December 1940.

Do 17s still took part in day attacks for all but one of the remaining days of August 1940. I and II./KG 3 attacked RAF Rochford in the afternoon of 28 August 1940, losing a 6 Staffel aircraft, while a 4 Staffel aircraft crashed back in France. I Gruppe lost two in accidents while on operations, involving the deaths of six crew members with another two wounded. Then on 30 August 1940, I./KG 76 attacked RAF Biggin Hill and, later, RAF Detling, but suffered no casualties.

The final day of August 1940, the 31st, was another one of good weather. That morning, II./KG 2 attacked RAF Duxford and III Gruppe went for RAF Debden. Casualties were light, with three wounded crew in total. Around midday it was the turn of I and II./KG 3 to target RAF Hornchurch, but four aircraft were shot down. The final Do 17 attack of the day was again against Hornchurch by KG 76; it involved fourteen aircraft from I Gruppe and four from III Gruppe. One Do 17 was lost and another damaged.

August 1940 had been a stern test for the Do 17 but from September 1940 onwards, there would be dramatic changes in the Luftwaffe's tactics.

Right: A battle formation of Do 17s is pictured en route to its target.

Above: Oberleutnant Rudolf Hallensleben, Staffelkapitän of 2./KG 76, is pictured in discussion with groundcrew beside one of his unit's Do 17Zs in August 1940. The distinctive 2 Staffel badge is very prominent. Hallensleben would be awarded the Ehrenpokal, Deutsches Kreuz in Gold and Ritterkreuz. He was killed near the war's end when his vehicle was strafed by American fighters near Leipheim in Bavaria on 19 April 1945.

Another Do 17Z of KG 76 is being prepared for its next mission. The lack of a badge and full code make it hard to identify the Gruppe or Staffel.

This heavily camouflaged Do 17Z, pictured in the summer of 1940, was being operated by 2./KG 3.

The band on the nose of this Do 17Z clearly denotes that it was a KG 2 aircraft. If the band was red, then this would signify II./KG 2; the colour apparently being applied to the spinners which would indicate 5./KG 2. Unfortunately, the badge is not clear enough for a positive identification. If it is the profile of a diving Dornier superimposed on a globe, then this would denote 5 Staffel. However, if the artwork shows a Middle Eastern man holding a telescope sitting on a bomb, then this would be 4./KG 2. However, just to confuse matters the latter badge has also been recorded on a Do 17Z of Stab/KG 2 which was brought down on 23 August 1940, crashing at Wickhambrook in Suffolk.

An unidentified Do 17Z which has suffered a starboard undercarriage collapse. This photograph was taken by a member of 3.(F)/123, a unit which did not operate the Do 17Z.

A meeting of types – in this case a Do 17Z of KG 76 and a Focke-Wulf Fw 200 of I./KG 40.

Coded 4U+BK, this particular aircraft was photographed in the summer of 1940. Interestingly, 2.(F)/123 had previously lost two Do 17Ps coded 4U+BK, on 31 October 1939 and 14 May 1940.

A nice air-to-air shot of a Do 17Z of unidentified unit that was taken in the summer of 1940.

A Do 17M of an unidentified reconnaissance unit. All that can be made out in terms of identification is a red letter 'E'.

An unusually angled photograph of a Do 17Z of Oberleutnant Helmut Powolny's 2./KG 2.

A Do 17P of 2.(F)/10 photographed in a camouflaged hay bale shelter at Saint-Inglevert in the summer of 1940.

Above: A Do 17Z of either II or III./KG 2; II Gruppe had a red band, while III Gruppe was denoted by a yellow band.

Right: The view from a Do 17Z en route to or from its target in August 1940. To the right can be made out at least two escorting Messerschmitt Bf 110s. Below these raiders is the distinctive stretch of the English coast at Eastbourne and Beachy Head.

A Do 17Z of II./KG 3 which appears to have suffered battle damage. Note how both tyres have burst, whilst there appears to be damage underneath the cockpit.

A Do 17Z of 9./KG 76, which appears to have adopted the former 5./KG 76 emblem.

A Do 17Z, believed to be from KG 3, is pictured being prepared for a mission in its revetment during the summer of 1940.

The crew of one Do 1Z from I./KG 2 pose for the camera with their senior mechanic in the summer of 1940.

A policeman surveys the wreckage of Do 17Z coded U5+KA which was shot down by a Spitfire, while attempting to bomb Eastchurch aerodrome, on the morning of 13 August 1940. With little option, the pilot, Oberleutnant Heinz Schlegel, selected an area of flat land near Barham, Kent, as a suitable spot to make a crash-landing. However, the Canterbury to Folkestone railway suddenly appeared in front of him. Having touched down, the Do 17 slammed into a tree and was torn in half; both sections came to rest on the railway itself by Pherbec Bridge.

Above: Bullet holes can be seen on the shattered rear fuselage of Do 17Z coded U5+KA as it lies beside the Canterbury to Folkestone railway line at Barham in Kent. Despite the scale of the damage to their aircraft, all four men on board, which aside from Schlegel included Oberleutnant Gerhard Oswald (Beobachter), Obergefreiter Gustav Babbe (Bordfunker) and Obergefreiter Ernst Holz (Bordmechaniker), survived. Schlegel was the only one found to be uninjured.

Right: The remains of the cockpit section of U5+KA resting beside the railway line at Pherbec Bridge near Barham in Kent. Schlegel had taken off from Saint-Léger at 06.30 hours. The Spitfire which attacked them, at about 08.30 hours, came out of the sun over the Thames Estuary and poured fire into the Dornier's tail and one of the engines. The ten 50kg bombs on board were immediately dropped blind.

Left: One of the men onboard U5+KA on the morning of 13 August 1940, was Oberleutnant Gerhard Oswald – seen here. Oswald was the Staffelkapitän of Stab/KG 2. He would spend the rest of the war in captivity.

Below: Another casualty of the aerial fighting on 13 August 1940. This is the wreckage of Do 17 U5+DS of 8./KG 2 which came down on the mudflats by the coastal village of Seasalter, to the west of Whitstable in Kent, at about 07.25 hours that morning.

A further view of the wreckage of U5+DS at Seasalter. Along with the rest of its Staffel, this aircraft had taken off from Douai at 07.00 hours. It was part of a formation of some forty raiders that had been tasked with attacking RAF Eastchurch.

Army personnel examine one of the engines of U5+DS on the mudflats at Seasalter. This aircraft was shot down by Hurricanes which attacked it at an altitude of 6,000ft.

Above: This picture showing one of the engines of U5+DS graphically illustrates the force of the impact when it crashed on 13 August 1940. The crew of U5+DS all baled out, but seemingly at too low an altitude for only one of the four, Feldwebel Rudolf Haensgen (Bordmechaniker), survived – he was captured wounded. The others, Oberleutnant Gerhard Müller (Flugzeugführer), Oberleutnant Werner Morich (Beobachter) and Oberfeldwebel Karl Langer (Bordfunker) were all killed. Langer's body was washed ashore at Gravesend nine days later.

Left: A soldier examines the machine-gun and turret ring of U5+DS on the mudflats at Seasalter.

The crew of a Do 17Z of 8./KG 76 check their flying clothing and equipment prior to taking-off for another flight. It would appear that many aircraft in this Staffel carried names; in this case *Elster* means 'Magpie'.

A formation of Do 17Zs over the UK in the summer of 1940. The aircraft coded F1+AB is from Stab I./KG 76 and is assumed to be that of either Major Theodore Schweitzer or Hauptmann Robert von Sichart.

The Ace of Hearts badge on the cowling identifies this crash-landed Do 17Z as being from 8./KG 3. The location and date are not known.

A dramatic photograph taken from a Do 17Z of 9./KG 76 on the afternoon of 16 August 1940. Just below the German bomber are ten RAF fighters climbing to intercept the incoming raid.

Do 17Zs over Southern England, almost certainly during the Battle of Britain. The unit is not known.

Not the best of photographs, but this image does show a Do 17Z of KG 76 fitted with a rear-facing flamethrower to ward off RAF fighters.

Left: Crews of KG 3 practising with flamethrowers at their base. The earlier flamethrower equipment fitted to the Do 17 was re-employed infantry weapons.

Above: Cleverly and courageously executed, the low-level attack by Dornier Do 17s against RAF Kenley on 18 August 1940 was one of the set-piece missions flown by the Luftwaffe on what has since become known as The Hardest Day. The Staffelkapitän of 9./KG 76 at the time of the raid was Hauptmann Joachim Roth, seen here on the telephone. An accomplished precision navigator, Roth would lead the Staffel to RAF Kenley with remarkable accuracy. Mist over the Channel and South Coast that morning had delayed the raid by a few hours and this photograph was taken as the unit had been relaxing whilst standing by for the word to go. Here, however, Roth is taking the call which informed him that the delayed operation had been given the green light. Seated at the table close to him, from left to right, are Oberleutnant Hermann Magin, Oberleutnant Hans-Siegfried Ahrends and Leutnant Wittman. Magin and Ahrends would both be killed on the Kenley mission, whilst Erwin Wittman survived, though badly wounded.

The Dornier Do 17Zs of III./KG 76 taking-off from Cormeilles-en-Vexin on Sunday, 18 August 1940.

Another image of Do 17Zs that was taken on 18 August 1940. In this case, it is the aircraft of 9./KG 76 that can be seen forming up before heading north across the Channel towards their targets in England.

Above: The view from Feldwebel Adolf Reichel's Do 17Z as it approaches the South Coast en route to Kenley on 18 August. Just ahead is the lead Kette comprising the three Do 17Zs flown by Oberleutnant Rudolf Lamberty, Unteroffizier Mathias Maasen and Feldwebel Wilhelm Raab.

Left: Seen through the ring-sight of a MG15 machine-gun, landfall on England's South Coast is just moments away for the Kenley raiders. The cliff directly ahead is Seaford Head in East Sussex. The lead aircraft is that flown by Oberleutnant Rudolf Lamberty.

The leading Kette is pictured streaking low over the waves past Beachy Head and its famous lighthouse. Moments later they would turn inland towards Kenley.

The Kenley force made landfall just east of Seaford in East Sussex – it was at about this moment that the picture seen here was taken.

Having just crossed the coast, the raiders hug the ground en route to Kenley. The town of Seaford can be seen just beyond Unteroffizier Günther Unger's Dornier Do 17Z at its station on the port outside of the formation. From the aircraft's shadow flitting across the fields below, the altitude of the aircraft can be estimated at around sixty feet.

Still hugging the terrain, the formation passes the rural Southease railway station which is located on the branch line between Lewes (to the north) and Seaford. (Courtesy of Andy Saunders)

Right: Another of the Kenley raiders' main turning points was Burgess Hill in West Sussex. This shot, taken from one of the Dorniers, shows Cyprus Road as people scurry for cover at 13.09 hours. The sandbagged building was the ARP centre and what appear to be tram lines are four newly laid strips of tarmac. As the raiders passed, so they machine-gunned various towns and villages.

Above: Kenley under attack on 18 August 1940. This picture of Spitfires and blast pens under fire was taken by Rolf von Pebal, a war photographer, who was in the aircraft flown by Feldwebel Adolf Reichel as it passed over the northern part of the airfield; the Spitfire is a 64 Squadron machine. This is a heavily retouched version that was used by German propaganda to present a more dramatic scene. This retouched version was, for example, published in *Der Adler*. The two largest clouds of smoke nearest the camera were not on the original. The smaller clouds beyond were and are probably the result of gunfire from the Do 17Z flown by Unteroffizier Günther Unger as it engaged a machine-gun post on the ground. (Historic Military Press)

Above: Smoke rising from the airfield at Kenley on 18 August 1940. The church that is visible in the foreground is St Andrew's in Coulsdon. It is reputed that the smoke from the attack was visible as far away as Brighton. (Historic Military Press)

Left: Buildings in East Grinstead photographed during the return flight from Kenley by war reporter Georg Hinze, who was in Oberleutnant Hermann Magin's crew. Their Do 17Z was in the third Kette during the attack on 18 August.

Above: One of the Kenley raiders which did not return on 18 August 1940. Pictured in the grounds of 'Sunnycroft', in Golf Road, Kenley, this is the wreckage of Oberleutnant Ahrend's Dornier Do 17Z-2, which, coded F1+HT, crashed at 13.20 hours on 18 August 1940. Mr Turner-Smith, who was in his house at the time, had a remarkable escape. 'I don't know why I am still alive.' He later told a reporter from the *Evening News*. His home was subsequently rebuilt. (Courtesy of Andy Saunders)

Right: Another view of the wreckage of Oberleutnant Ahrend's Do 17Z under RAF guard. This aircraft had been caught either by Kenley's Parachute and Cable defences, light anti-aircraft fire, or both, causing it to crash at 'Sunnycroft'. All four crew men on board, as well as Oberst Dr Sommer, were killed. (Courtesy of Andy Saunders)

Above: Coded F1+DT, this is the Dornier Do 17Z-2 of 9./KG 76, flown by Oberleutnant Rudolf Lamberty and his crew, pictured after it crashed at Leaves Green near Biggin Hill at about 13.30 hours. Fire quickly took hold in the already burning aircraft after it had come to a rest and all of the five men on board were taken prisoner, albeit injured.

Left: Oberleutnant Rudolf Lamberty, seen here, survived the events of 18 August 1940. Normally, the Do 17 carried a crew of four, but a fifth man, Hauptmann Gustav Peters, was also on board Lamberty's aircraft that day. Peters had gone along to gain experience of low-level operations. Lamberty and his navigator, Hauptmann Joachim Roth, the Staffelkapitän, were both burned in the crash landing.

Feldwebel Adolf Reichel's Do 17Z after its crash-landing near Abbeville on the return from Kenley.

A second view of Feldwebel Adolf Reichel's crash-landed Do 17Z on 18 August 1940.

Left: Feldwebel Günther Unger of 9./KG 76 was forced to ditch in the Channel on the return flight from Kenley on 18 August. Unger himself later recalled the following: 'We had been quite badly hit by the fighters and ground fire, one way and another. I had one engine out and feathered the propeller. One of the hits had severed a fuel pipe and petrol had started to leak into the cockpit. The observer broke open the first aid kit and bound up the leak with sticking plaster. Luckily, though, nobody was wounded. About five miles from the coast the fighters broke off their attacks … Then we were over the sea just as the life-saving engine packed up again. Now we were at 200 metres and heading slowly back home although the remaining engine was getting hotter and hotter and then, within sight of France, it began to misfire. Desperately, I tried again to re-start the starboard engine. But it was no good. Finally, the port motor gave up as well.' Moments later his aircraft hit the water.

Above: A heavily camouflaged Do 17Z of 9./KG 76 at Cormeilles-en-Vexin. The individual on the left is Feldwebel Günther Unger – one of the Kenley raiders.

Above: Four members of 9./KG 76 – Oberleutnant Rudolf Lamberty (PoW in the raid on Kenley on 18 August), Oberleutnant Ahrends (killed), Oberleutnant Hermann Magin (died of wounds), and Hauptmann Joachim Roth (PoW) – dine together on the eve of their fateful mission against RAF Kenley on 18 August 1940. (Courtesy of Andy Saunders)

Right: A Do 17Z of 9./KG 76 that carries an alternative unit emblem that was adopted after the Battle of France.

A Do 17Z of KG 76 showing the results of being attacked by an RAF fighter.

This is reputed to be a photograph showing the last moments of the Do 17Z of I./KG 76 that was shot down by Pilot Officer Alan Eckford of 32 Squadron on 18 August 1940, and which crashed at Hurst Green.

This heavily armed Do 17 of an unidentified units appears to have suffered considerable damage under the nose.

An RAF NCO points at the swastika on the tail of Dornier Do 17Z-3 5K+AP which crashed at Bilsby in Lincolnshire at 14.30 hours on 21 August 1940. One of three aircraft of 6/KG 3 tasked with attacking a convoy, it collided with the port aircraft in the formation having flown into cloud to evade RAF fighters. The other Do 17Z, coded 5K+BP, also came down near Bilsby.

The shattered cockpit section of 5K+AP. Two of those on board, Oberleutnant Herbert Schwartz (Staffelkapitän) and Oberleutnant Ulrich Matschoss, survived the collision. The other two, Oberfeldwebel Wilhelm Loos and Unteroffizier Helmut Lehman, were killed. Both men now lie in Cannock Chase German Military Cemetery.

An official photograph taken by a Dornier Flugzeugwerke photographer during August 1940. Some two months later, production of the 'Flying Pencil' would cease.

Major Martin Gutzmann, the Gruppenkommandeur of I./KG 2, had only just returned to the unit, having been convalescing after being wounded on 10 May 1940, when he was shot down on 26 August 1940. At the time, Gutzmann was involved in an attack on RAF Hornchurch. As this picture of his aircraft, Do 17Z-3 W.Nr. 2425 and coded U5+GK, shows, he managed to execute a good belly-landing. The actual spot was some two miles south-west of Eastchurch in Kent.

The cockpit section of Gutzmann's U5+GK after its belly-landing on 26 August 1940. Having bombed RAF Hornchurch, Gutzmann's aircraft turned for home. However, one of the engines began to play up, causing U5+GK to fall behind the rest of the formation. It was then set upon by a number of Spitfires, in which onslaught both of the engines were put out of action. The Bordmechaniker of his crew, Gutzmann, like Unteroffizier Ambrosius Schmelzer (Flugzeugführer) and Unteroffizier Helmut Buhr (Bordmechaniker), was uninjured in the combat and subsequent crash. The Bordfunker, Oberleutnant Siegfried Hertel, was killed – presumably by the fighter attacks.

Looking down on the cockpit of U5+GK – a picture which clearly illustrates how cramped and confined the space was. The addition of two extra side guns would only have exacerbated the situation.

Do 17P 5D+JL, an aircraft of 3.(F)/31, had been tasked with a reconnaissance sortie over Plymouth when it was shot down by a pair of Spitfires of 238 Squadron on 27 August 1940. It came down at Hardwick Farm, Tavistock, at 10.30 hours. The airframe was duly recovered and put on public display in Salisbury – when this photograph was taken.

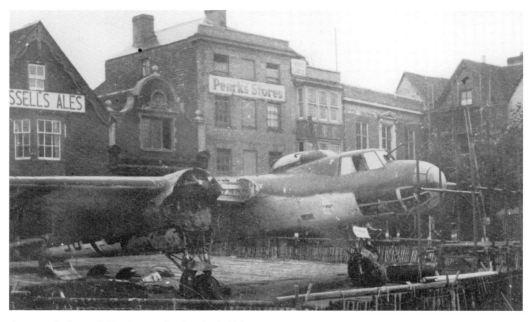

A second view of 5D+JL on display in Salisbury. Intercepted at an altitude of 16,000ft, one of the engines failed, forcing the pilot to make an emergency landing. The two Spitfires involved were flown by Squadron Leader Minden Blake and Pilot Officer Brian Considine.

Left: The last of our trio of images of 5D+JL in Salisbury. Prior to being put on public show, this aircraft had been taken to RAE Farnborough for evaluation and examination. The crew comprised Leutnant Walter Haffa (Flugzeugführer), Feldwebel Gustav Klauschenke (Beobachter) and Gefreiter Johannes Schlesiel (Bordfunker), all of whom were captured.

Above: A handwritten note on the rear of this photograph states that it shows a 'Dornier Do 17 having been assembled at Dean Park cricket ground, Bournemouth, in association with Hampshire Spitfire Fund, summer 1940'. Note the member of the Home Guard on the left. The aircraft is, once again, 5D+JL which features in the previous three images. One source states that the Dornier was 'reassembled and transported to the County Cricket Ground in Bournemouth and then on to Salisbury'. (Historic Military Press)

Above: Seen here in the centre, Graf von Platen-Hallermund was killed when his Do 17Z-3 of 1./KG 3, W.Nr. 2807 and coded 5K+JH, crashed near Chêne al Pierre on 28 August 1940. His Beobachter, Feldwebel Hermann Köhler (right), also lost his life. The other two crew members, Unteroffizier Hans Fedder (Bordmechaniker) and Unteroffizier Kurt Ohlsen (Bordfunker), were both injured.

Right: Unteroffizier Reiner usually flew with Oberleutnant Rudolf Graf von Platen-Hallermund. He undoubtedly had a lucky escape on 28 August 1940.

Left: Mirroring scenes that would be seen on the opposite side of the Channel, here members of a Lufwaffe salvage team are at work recovering a crash-landed Do 17Z.

Above: The wreckage of Do 17Z-3, W.Nr. 2669, pictured burning furiously on the beach at Sandwich, Kent, on 31 August 1940. Coded 5K+LM, this 4./KG 3 aircraft was part of a force despatched to attack an RAF airfield to the east of London. Having bombed the target, the raiders were promptly engaged by defending fighters. Such was the damage to 5K+LM, that its pilot was forced to put his aircraft on the wide expanse of Sandwich Flats. Having come to a halt some 200 yards from the Princess Golf Club, its crew, Oberfeldwebel Willi Lange (Flugzeugführer), Unteroffizier Fritz Kostropetsch (Beobachter), Feldwebel Hubert Berndt (Bordfunker) and Feldwebel Hans Wünsch (Bordmechaniker), set fire to it. All four were captured wounded.

Like Oberfeldwebel Lange's crew in 5K+LM, that of Leutnant Josef Kleppmeier, in Do 17Z coded F1+BK, and which had the W.Nr. 3316, had also dropped their bombs and had turned for home when they were intercepted by some eight RAF fighters on 31 August 1940. With one engine hit, Kleppmeier was left with little choice to put his 2./KG 76 aircraft down, which he did at Newchurch near Dungeness.

Kleppmeier's crash-landing left F1+BK badly damaged. Kleppmeier, however, was the only occupant not to be injured. His three crew mates, Feldwebel Harald Pfaehler (Beobachter), Unteroffizier Albert Bloss (Bordfunker) and Oberfeldwebel Heinrich Lang (Bordmechaniker), were all wounded, some severely. It was noted that the aircraft had the usual 2./KG 76 badge on the nose of a bomb falling on a lion.

The wing of a badly damaged Do 17Z of 6./KG 2. Note the daylight formation marking obscuring the wing cross.

A Do 17Z of 1./KG 76, that coded F1+HH, pictured with the rest of its formation over the UK in the summer of 1940. Note the red devil badge and white spinners of 1./KG 76.

AUGUST 1940

This shot, presumably taken moments after the previous image, shows the crew of F1+HH releasing a 50kg bomb on its target.

A view of the same formation that includes F1+HH en route to, or returning from, a mission in the summer of 1940.

Above: This Do 17Z of of 1./KG 76, in this case that which is coded F1+CH, has been photographed getting pretty close to his Kette leader.

Left: A close-up of the cockpit section of a Do 17 of 1./KG 76 which clearly shows the Staffel emblem.

Major Klaus Uebe (on the left) took command of III./KG 2 after Major Adolf Fuchs was wounded on 31 August 1940. He handed over to Major Friedrich Dreyer on 20 March 1941.

Chapter 3

September and October 1940

September 1940 began badly for KG 76 with a number of aircraft being damaged during attacks on RAF Kenley, RAF Biggin Hill and RAF Gravesend. The only loss came from 9 Staffel and resulted in Oberfeldwebel Wilhelm Illg being captured. Illg had previously been awarded the Ritterkreuz for flying back a Do 17Z with a mortally wounded pilot on 18 August 1940.

Following an attack on RAF Eastchurch on 2 September, III./KG 3 suffered two aircraft destroyed on returning to the Continent, while an aircraft from 9./KG 76 crash-landed on Rochford airfield. I./KG 76 was also recorded as having attacked RAF Hornchurch on this date. The following morning II./KG 2 attacked RAF North Weald losing one from 5./KG 2.

It appears that the Do 17 Geschwader were taking turns in attacking airfields as I./KG 76 attacked RAF Rochford on 4 September 1940. The day after saw an increase in tempo with II./KG 2 attacking RAF Biggin Hill in the late morning, while, that evening, a number of Geschwader, including KG 2, KG 3 and I./KG 76, targeted oil tanks at Thameshaven and London Docks; the only casualties were two aircraft from 6./KG 2 damaged attacking Biggin Hill.

Little action was recorded the following day and that night, aside from the fact that I./KG 76 again attacked Thameshaven.

A major change in German tactics then followed on 7 September 1940. On what was the first day of the Blitz, British airfields were now secondary to attacks on London and other major cities. This development marked the start of the beginning of the end for massed daylight attacks by Do 17s.

All three Do 17 Geschwader were in action that day. II and III./KG 2 attacked Victoria Docks; two aircraft returned with wounded crew. An aircraft of 4./KG 2 crashed in France killing all the crew. KG 3 had six aircraft from II and III Gruppe damaged over London and one aircraft from Stab./KG 3 came down in the Channel. The only Do 17Z to crash in the UK did so early that evening when a Stab/KG 76 aircraft, tasked with photographing damage from the earlier attack, was attacked by a Spitfire from 234 Squadron. The latter itself was then damaged, following which the two aircraft collided and crashed.

The following day saw a spectacular loss. II./KG 2 took off for London only to be recalled due to weather. They took off again just over an hour later together with

III Gruppe. As they approached London, an aircraft of 5./KG 2 took a direct hit from anti-aircraft fire and exploded, mortally damaging two more aircraft, while a fourth aircraft was damaged. The only other Do 17 losses of the day were a mid-air collision over Belgium between two aircraft of 3./KG 3.

With the return of bad weather, the only Do 17 loss for the next six days was one of 9./KG 76's aircraft on 10 September 1940. The culmination of daylight attacks now came on 15 September 1940. II and III./KG 2 lost seven aircraft on what is now known as Battle of Britain Day (with many others returning damaged). II./KG 3 lost six aircraft with a number returning damaged and KG 76 lost six aircraft.

It was following this that the Luftwaffe was forced to stop deploying the Do 17Z as part of massed daylight raids, such were the losses being suffered by all three bomber units. From this point on, the Do 17Z would be employed more at night, or at the hands of experienced crews who would use bad weather and low-level flight to attack specific targets by day.

The days that followed saw very few Do 17 combat losses. On 20 September 1940, a Do 17P of 4.(F)/121 returned damaged by fighters, and, the day after, two aircraft from Küstenfliegergruppe 606 crashed returning from a night attack on Liverpool.

What was now starting to occur more often were lone aircraft carrying out nuisance attacks. By means of an example, on 19 September, a lone aircraft from Küstenfliegergruppe 606 attacked RAF St Eval, while on 24 September, one from 2./KG 76 attacked London using the cloud as a means of defence. This aircraft was, however, damaged by Hurricanes from 605 Squadron and force-landed near Boulogne. Only one more Do 17Z was lost on operations in September 1940 – an aircraft from 8./KG 3 which crashed in the Channel on the last day of the month.

With October 1940 came poorer weather and a reduction in losses. For example, KG 2 reported the total loss of just seven Do 17 during the month. Of those, one was lost to anti-aircraft fire, five were the result of accidents and one on daylight operations.

Küstenfliegergruppe 606 did have some continued success with its nuisance attacks. For example, at dawn on 3 October 1940, three aircraft carried out a successful attack on St Eval, while the following day, a similar raid was carried out against the airfield at Penrhos in Wales. Again, the attacks by this unit did not go without a cost; eight aircraft were lost on operations in October 1940. At the start of 1941, Küstenfliegergruppe 606 began converting to the Ju 88.

Towards the end of October 1940, the Luftwaffe tried a new tactic. Under the code name *Opernball*, aircraft flown by experienced crews either individually or in threes carried out low-level raids normally at dawn or dusk and in poor weather conditions against Bomber Command airfields – the so-called and termed Zerstörerangriffe attacks. KG 2 attacked RAF Honington, RAF Newmarket and RAF Mildenhall on 27 October 1940, while two days later 8./KG 2 attacked Newmarket and 6./KG 2 struck at RAFWattisham. However, such attacks did not go without casualties.

With the end of the Battle of Britain and the Blitz underway, it was clear that the future of the Do 17 was coming to an end. *But there was little or no future for the Flying Pencil.*

DORNIER Do 17 IN THE BATTLE OF BRITAIN

In June 1940, a night fighter unit designated Nachtjagdgeschwader 1 was formed and as an interim measure, two versions of the Do 17 named the Z-7 Kauz I and the Z-10 Kauz II (Kauz meaning Screech Owl) were introduced. The nose was removed from a Do 17Z-3 and replaced by the nose from a Ju 88C fighter armed with three 7.9mm machine-guns and one 20mm cannon. This was soon found to be unsatisfactory, and a new nose was designed which increased the armament to four machine-guns and two cannon. In the tip of the nose was an infra-red spotlight which was later replaced by first-generation radar and was designated the Do 17Z-10.

Just two were lost in accidents in the period of the Battle of Britain. At the same time, only four claims were made by their crews, of which two were the result of engagements over mainland Britain.

If there was any doubt that the Do 17's future was short-lived, this was dispelled by the news that production of the type ceased in October. By this point, some 500 Do 17Z-1 and Z-2 and 22 Z-3 aircraft had been built; the total of all types built has been stated as being 2,139.

Above: Marking a dramatic change in the Luftwaffe's tactics, here Do 17Zs of III./KG 2 are pictured heading for London on 7 September 1940, the opening day of the Blitz. It was at 16.43 hours that the sirens in London sounded on that fateful Saturday. Once the first bombs started falling, the raid lasted for approximately an hour, the 'All Clear' being sounded at 18.10 hours. During those frantic sixty or so minutes the devastation wrought of parts of London by the first wave of bombers had been enormous. Factory buildings had been demolished, hundreds of tons of timber had been left in charred ruins, warehouses filled with foodstuffs and other supplies vital to the war effort had gone up in smoke and the houses of the dockers and the little corner shops that fed them had collapsed into rubble.

Dornier Do 17Zs of KG 3 over London on September 7. The white bar on the wings possibly denotes that they are from I Gruppe. Beneath them lies London's Silvertown, with West Ham speedway in Canning Town clearly visible in the centre of the image. Smoke from the fires that have been started either side of the Royal Victoria Dock can also be seen in the bottom right.

Above: A Do 17Z, believed to be from KG 3, under attack. Note how the port engine has been feathered and is smoking.

Left: A pair of Do 17s, those coded U5+AP and U5+CP, of Oberleutnant Gerhard Czernik's 6./KG 2 photographed over water, presumably the English Channel, on their way to their target. The Do 17Z coded U5+CP and which had the W.Nr. 2785 suffered 35% damage when it collided with an RAF fighter over London on 8 September 1940.

Do 17Z U5+HT, of 9./KG 2, is pictured here at Coquelles in the summer of 1940. It has obviously been engaged in combat, though the damage is slight.

Do 17Zs of 1./KG 76 braving the skies of southern England in the summer of 1940.

Left: Flak bursts above a Do 17Z of 1./KG 76 during a raid over London or the South East in September 1940. There are vapour trails above the flak bursts.

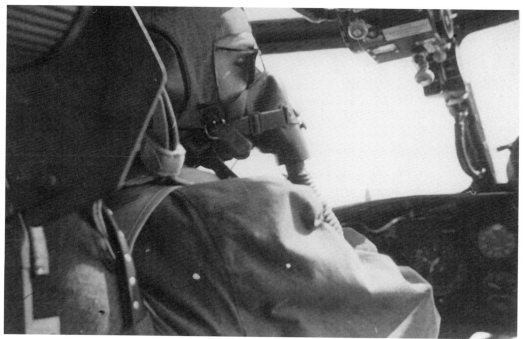

Above: Leutnant Josef Steudel of 8./KG 2 photographed at the controls of his Do 17Z over London on the second day of the Blitz – 8 September 1940.

Opposite above: This image of Unteroffizier Gotthardt Wachtel, the Bordfunker in Leutnant Josef Steudel's 8./KG 2 crew, was again taken whilst his Do 17 was over London on 8 September 1940.

Opposite below: Unteroffizier Karl Steigemann, Leutnant Josef Steduel's Bordmechaniker, again pictured on 8 September. Steigemann would be killed in an accident whilst flying with another crew on 30 September that year.

Vapour trails from RAF fighters seen from a Do 17Z of 8./KG 2 whilst it was over London on 8 September 1940.

Coded T6+FA, this Do 17P is from Stab./StG 2. A Do 17P-2 with this code, and W.Nr. 4041, was lost in Greece, whilst being operated by StG 2, on 11 April 1941.

This Do 17, coded 4N+CK, is from 2.(F)/22, which was based at Stavanger-Sola from August 1940 whilst converting to the Ju 88. This aircraft, which probably had the W.Nr. 3519, suffered an accident at Stavanger on 14 September 1940, after which it was written off. (via Maesel)

Photographed at Brest-Süd, this is a Do 17Z-5 of 1./Küstenfliegergruppe 606. With the W.Nr. 1213, and coded 7T+BH, it suffered a collapsed undercarriage on 14 September 1940.

Above: The crew of Feldwebel Karl Niebler pictured in the foreground beside their aircraft from 2./KG 76, Do 17Z-3 W.Nr. 2651 and coded F1+FL, shortly before take-off from Beauvais on the morning of 15 September 1940. Left to right are Niebler (Flugzeugführer), Oberleutnant Karl-Ernst Wilke (Beobachter), Feldwebel Karl-Heinz Wissmann (Bordschütze), their leading ground mechanic, Unteroffizier Johann-Friedrich Schatz (Bordschütze), and Unteroffizier Hans Zrenner (Bordfunker). By about 12.30 hours, this aircraft had been shot down by Spitfires, crashing at Sturry in Kent. Only Wilke and Zrenner survived, though both were injured.

Left: This 2./KG 76 crew managed to get back to Beauvais in their damaged Do 17Z, which had the code letter F1+EK. The crew comprised Feldwebel Theo Rehm (Beobachter), Feldwebel Eikelmann (Bordmechaniker), Unteroffizier Hans-Joachim Hanke (Flugzeugführer) and Unteroffizier Schulz (Bordfunker).

One of the seriously injured crew members of Do 17Z, W.Nr. 2555 and coded F1+FS, is carried away from his 8./KG 76 aircraft at Lullingstone in Kent. This raider had been shot down at 12.10 hours during an attack on London on 15 September 1940. The victors on this occasion were Flying Officer John Dundas and Pilot Officer Eugene 'Red' Tobin of 609 (West Riding) Squadron.

Work to dismantle F1+FS at Lullingstone Castle Farm gets underway. The crew were Feldwebel Rolf Heitsch (Flugzeugführer), Feldwebel Hans Pfeiffer (Bordfunker), Feldwebel Martin Sauter (Bordmechaniker) and Feldwebel Stephan Schmid (Beobachter). They were all captured, though all but Heitsch had been wounded. Schmid was so badly injured that he died shortly after his Do 17 had crashed.

Above: A report made following an examination of F1+FS at Lullingstone Castle Farm notes that the second 'F' of the code letters was outlined in white, that there was a red band around the fuselage, red spinners and a horizontal pink band on the outside of the rudders. The 8./KG 76 badge of three white bombers on a red bomb and black shield was present on the nose.

Left: This camera gun still, taken by Pilot Officer Keith Ogilvie of 609 (West Riding) Squadron, shows a Do 17 of KG 76. It was probably taken on 15 September 1940. Visible is the fuselage band and day formation markings on the wing tip.

Opposite above: One of the most iconic pictures to emerge from the Battle of Britain, this image shows the final moments of Do 17Z W.Nr. 2361, coded of F1+FH of 1./KG 76, which broke up over London on 15 September 1940. This loss was claimed by countless RAF pilots, including Flight Lieutenant Jerrard Jeffries, Sergeant Josef Hubacek, Sergeant Raimund Puda, and Sergeant Jan Kaucky of 310 (Czech) Squadron, Pilot Officer Johnnie Curchin and Pilot Officer Keith Ogilvie of 609 (West Riding) Squadron, and Flying Officer Trevor Parsons of 504 Squadron. The stricken aircraft may also have been fired on by Pilot Officer Arthur Cochrane of 257 Squadron. It was finally finished off by Sergeant Ray Holmes of 504 Squadron.

Opposite below: F1+FH had taken off earlier that day from its base at Nivelles just south of Beauvais at 10.05 hours. Twenty-seven-year-old Oberleutnant Robert Zehbe was at the controls. It ended its flight scattered over Central London. The wreckage seen here fell just outside Victoria Railway Station. Zehbe was killed that day. As for the rest of his crew of Unteroffizier Hans Goschenhofer (Beobachter), Unteroffizier Gustav Hubel (Bordschütze), Unteroffizier Leo Hammermeister (Bordmechaniker), and Obergefreiter Ludwig Armbruster (Bordfunker), only last two survived. (Historic Military Press)

DORNIER Do 17 IN THE BATTLE OF BRITAIN

A pair of Do 17Zs of 4./KG 3 in the summer of 1940. Nearest the camera is 5K+AM. If this aircraft had the W.Nr. 2879, then it was the 5K+AM that was badly damaged in combat on 15 September 1940. Despite the crew's best efforts to reach an airfield, they crash-landed at Mardyck near Dunkirk.

This Do 17Z-3 is 5K+AM pictured having just managed to make it back to the Continent and crash-land following its sortie as part of the late afternoon attack on London on 15 September 1940. A 4./KG 3 aircraft, it had the W.Nr. 2879.

With its starboard engine stopped and port engine struggling, Leutnant Sieghard Schopper managed to crash-land 5K+AM on or near the sand dunes at Mardyck.

Above: German personnel pose for the camera in the battered cockpit of 5K+AM after its crash-landing on the afternoon of 15 September 1940.

Left: As well as Schopper, the crew of 5K+AM also included Oberleutnant Bernhard Granicky (Beobachter; and Staffelkapitän), Feldwebel Felix Gwidziel (Bordfunker) and Feldwebel Heinz Kirch (Bordmechaniker). Schopper and Granicky were uninjured, while the other two were slightly wounded.

The losses for the Do 17 units on 15 September 1940 continued to mount – as the following series of ten images depicting Do 17Z coded F1+JK testify.

Having been crippled by the RAF fighters or anti-aircraft over London or southern England, F1+JK's pilot, Unteroffizier Hans Figge, managed to nurse his stricken Do 17 back across the Channel, getting as far inland as five miles north of Poix before crash-landing. Some of the crew can be seen standing on the cockpit roof.

Aside from Figge, the other members of F1+JK's crew were Oberleutnant Martin Florian (Beobachter), who was slightly wounded, Unteroffizier Wagner (Bordfunker) and Obergefreiter Sommer (Bordmechaniker).

Here a bandaged member of Figge's crew can be seen enjoying a much-needed drink while standing beside the cockpit of F1+JK. Presumably, based on the information in the previous caption, it is Oberleutnant Martin Florian who is pictured here.

Among the damage inflicted on F1+JK, it was the fact that one of the engines had stopped that forced Figge to consider a crash-landing. This was well executed however, allowing the crew to clamber out once the air frame had come to a halt.

All four members of Figge's crew pictured after their arrival back in France – all four no doubt relieved to have survived the ordeal they had just endured.

Above: Members of F1+JK's crew gather around the battered nose section in the aftermath of their crash-landing. Oberleutnant Martin Florian can be seen in the centre looking up at the camera.

Left: Evidence of fighter attacks is clearly visible on F1+JK's port wing.

Similar bullet holes also litter F1+JK's fuselage.

A photograph of the interior of F1+JK after its crash-landing near Poix on 15 September 1940.

Yet another Do 17 that, damaged in the aerial battles on 15 September 1940, only just made it back across the Channel. This Do 17Z-3 of 8./KG 2, W.Nr. 2644, crash-landed on the beach at Berck.

With the sand dunes as a backdrop, this is another view of the Do 17Z-3, W.Nr. 2644, which came down at Berck on 15 September. The pilot, Leutnant Wilhelm Schenke, was uninjured. However, the rest of the crew, Unteroffizier Gerhard Heinz (Beobachter), Unteroffizier Ludiwig Sturm (Bordfunker) and Oberfeldwebel Fritz Winkler (Bordmechaniker) were all wounded.

This photograph, dated 21 September 1940, features the shattered remains of one Do 17. Just visible are the code letters CL. This is a Do 17Z-5 of 3./ Küstenfliegergruppe 606 which had the W.Nr. 3471. It crashed a couple of miles south of Landernau in Brittany while returning from a night-time sortie. Unteroffizier Otto Von Bock und Plach (Flugzeugführer), Oberleutnant zS Eberhard von Krosigk (Beobachter) and Unteroffizier Bruno Richter (Bordmechaniker) were killed, whilst the Bordfunker baled out and landed safely.

During a combat patrol on 24 September 1940, Pilot Officer Witold Glowacki and Flying Officer Ian Muirhead, both flying Hurricanes of 605 (County of Warwick) Squadron, encountered and pursued a Do 17Z of 2./KG 76. The bomber had the W.Nr. 3317 and was coded F1+GK. The attacks on the bomber were sufficient enough to cause its pilot to crash-land near Boulogne – following which this and the next photograph were taken. The Flugzeugführer, Unteroffizier Hans Figge (who, as we have seen, also crash-landed on 15 September 1940), was uninjured, while his Bordmechaniker, Unteroffizier Gottfried Curth, was slightly wounded.

Another of the crash-landed F1+GK near Boulogne. On this occasion the two victors did not have long to celebrate their 'kill'. Turning for home Glowacki and Muirhead were, in turn, 'bounced' by Bf 109s (some accounts give the number as three) from 3./JG 51. Having run out of ammunition, the two Hurricanes were unable to properly defend themselves, in which state Glowacki was shot down by Oberleutnant Michael Sonner. Glowacki force-landed P3832 near Ambleteuse. Although pictures taken in the immediate aftermath of his crash show that Glowacki had been captured alive, albeit with his head bandaged, he died later the same day – possibly from a severe reaction to an anti-tetanus injection. He is buried in Guines Communal Cemetery, France. Muirhead, for his part, was able to make it back to Croydon. He was killed in action on 15 October 1940.

Even the nose band of this Do 17Z of KG 2 has been toned down for operations during the Blitz.

With the code 5K+FA, this Do 17Z of Stab/KG 3 was photographed at some point in the summer of 1940. On its nose is the red and white arms of the town of Elbing. The Do 17Z-3 that carried the W.Nr. 2491 and codes 5K+FA crashed near Maastricht when the crew became disorientated during an operational flight on 26 September 1940.

A Do 17P pictured in a former Armée de l'Air hangar alongside a Stuka of StG 2. The last two digits of the W.Nr. suggest that this aircraft was 1096, which, serving with 4.(F)/14, was lost in an accident near Plumetot on 29 September 1940.

Above: A Do 17Z of unidentified unit pictured together with its escort in the summer of 1940.

Left: The bullet-riddled wreckage of Do 17Z-3, W.Nr. 2822 and coded 5K+GR, of 7./KG 3 pictured lying on the beach at Boulogne on 30 September 1940.

Above: The partially burnt out
remains of Oberleutnant Hans
Langer's Do 17Z, W.Nr. 3423
and U5+FA of Stab/KG 2, after
being shot down by 17 Squadron
on 2 October 1940. It came down
at Rookery Farm, Cretingham,
Suffolk, at 10.20 hours, having been
tasked to undertake a weather and
photographic reconnaissance flight.

Right: Oberleutnant Hans Langer
pictured as he passed through one
of London's railway stations, under
guard, on his way to captivity.

A formation of Do 17Zs of II./KG 2 in the summer of 1940. The aircraft nearest the camera would appear to be coded U5+DM, while next to it is U5+KM. Both were aircraft of 4./KG 2. The crew of the U5+DM which had the W.Nr. 2659, and which may be the aircraft seen here, baled out from their aircraft near Paris, after it had suffered damage from anti-aircraft fire, on 2 October 1940.

Another Do 17Z-5 of Küstenfliegergruppe 606 that suffered a landing accident at Brest-Süd. This aircraft has the W.Nr. 2530; the incident in question occurred on 3 October 1940.

A Do 17Z-5 of Küstenfliegergruppe 606 being recovered by a Luftwaffe salvage team following its crash-landing near Brest in October. Note the jacking points over the wings.

A Do 17Z coded U5+BM of Oberleutnant Joachim Genzow's 4./KG 2 pictured releasing its deadly cargo on an unfortunate target in the summer of 1940. If this aircraft had the W.Nr 1201, then it was the U5+BM that crashed at Saint-Léger, due to engine failure, on 10 October 1940.

Another view of bombs falling away from the Do 17Z coded U5+BM. The replacement U5+BM, for that lost on 10 October 1940, had the W.Nr. 3495. The latter survived for less than a month. Hit by anti-aircraft fire, it crashed off Walmer Beach at 20.40 hours on 9 November 1940. Leutnant Günter Mollenhauer and his crew were all killed.

A Do 17Z of an unidentified unit getting airborne for a night attack during the Blitz. Note, once again, how all the markings have been painted over.

A Do 17Z-5 of 1./ Küstenfliegergruppe 606. Note the Küstenfliegergruppe 606 badge over an eagle pecking a depiction of Britain. The only aircraft recorded with this code of 7T+HH had the W.Nr. 2787; it was damaged in combat during an attack on Liverpool on 11 October 1940.

Another view of Do 17Z-5 7T+HH of 1./Küstenfliegergruppe 606 – note the blacked-out markings. As mentioned, this aircraft was attacked by Spitfires of 611 (West Lancashire) Squadron whilst attacking Liverpool on 11 October 1940; more specifically, it was probably damaged by Flight Lieutenant Bill Leather. Some of the results of Leather's fire can clearly be seen.

The rear fuselage of Do 17Z-5 7T+HH showing more of the damage caused by the attacking Spitfires on 11 October 1940. With two engines on fire, two of the Dornier's crew, Feldwebel Willi Staas (Bordfunker) and Unteroffizier Heinz Johannsen (Bordmechaniker), baled out near Capel Curig in North Wales. Johannsen is believed to have hit the tail as he was found dead at Deiniolen, seven miles east of Caernarvon with an unopened parachute. Staas landed safely and was quickly captured.

The tail section of Do 17Z-5 7T+HH. At the time it was believed that, with Staas and Johannsen having baled out, their Do 17 had crashed 'somewhere in the wilds of North Wales', and that the two remaining crew members, Oberfeldwebel Willi Hagen (Flugzeugführer) and Oberleutnant zS Karl-Franz Heine (Beobachter), were missing. However, Hagen had managed to nurse the crippled Do 17 back to land at Brest. The damage visible to the tail in this picture almost certainly provides a tragic clue to the fate that befall Heinz Johannsen.

Leutnant Josef Steudel (second from right) and his 8./KG 2 crew pictured at Cambrai-Süd in August 1940.

Leutnant Josef Steudel's Do 17Z W.Nr. 3432 was damaged in combat with a Hurricane of 213 Squadron – that flown by Dennis David – on 19 October 1940. This picture was taken after it had managed to land back at Cambrai.

Above: The cockpit section of Steudel's Do 17Z pictured after the combat on 19 October 1940.

Left and below: Effects of the RAF attacks clearly visible on Steudel's Do 17Z. Luftwaffe records indicate that the aircraft suffered 40% damage in the Hurricanes' fire.

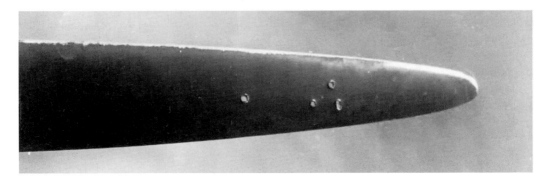

Right: Work begins
to recover Leutnant
Steudel's Do 17Z at
Cambrai in October
1940.

Above: On the night of 21 October 1940, Leutnant Walter Stirnat and his crew of 1./
Küstenfliegergruppe 606, flying Do 17Z-5, W.Nr 2783 and coded 7T+AH , became lost on
operations over the west of England. Eventually, thinking that they were over France, the four
men on board baled out over Salisbury Plain and were all captured. Their aircraft flew on until it
came down on the mud flats near Shotley in Essex – where this image was taken. A subsequent
intelligence report noted the presence of a unit badge of an eagle holding the British Isles in its
claws and the fitment of two streamlined bulges either side of the nose. The latter were flotation
pods which contained inflatable rubber buoys.

Two Do 17Zs of KG 76 seen over England during October 1940. Neither have been camouflaged for night operations.

Groundcrew busy applying night camouflage to tone down the markings and fuselage of a Do 17Z of KG 76 during the Blitz.

Hastily applied camouflage to a Do 17Z of 8./KG 3 late in 1940. Note the blinds in the cockpit.

A Do 17Z of 1./KG 2 showing clearly its eagle and bomb badge. This picture was taken at Épinoy in late 1940. All other markings have been painted over. (via Oliver)

Above: Though many of the surfaces and markings on this Do 17Z have been overpainted, the unit's emblem has been left untouched. The green dragon in fact identifies this aircraft as being from 7./KG 76.

Left: This Do 17Z, coded U5+EH, of Hauptmann Hans-Uwe Ortmann's 1./KG 2 had tipped over at Grevelliers in late 1940. Note the partial toning down of the fuselage and markings.

A Do 17Z of an unidentified unit over its target, with bomb doors open, in late 1940.

This Do 17Z of 5./KG 2, coded U5+AN, taxied into a bomb crater at Cambrai-Sud having returned from an attack on London on the night of 27 October 1940. The crew was made up of Unteroffizier Ernst Fröhlich (Bordfunker; PoW on 15 May 1944), Leutnant Karl Manowarda (Flugzeugführer; also PoW on 15 May 1944), Oberfeldwebel Helmut Petraschke (Beobachter), and Unteroffizier Ernst Geselle (Bordmechaniker; killed on 25 June 1942).

Chapter 4

Dornier Do 17 Aircraft Casualties

Date	Unit	Type	W/NR	SKZ	Codes	Duty
3.7.1940	2.(F)/123	Do 17 P				Operational
3.7.1940	Stab./ KG 2	Do 17 Z			U5+EA	Operational
3.7.1940	3./KG 3	Do 17 Z				Operational
3.7.1940	1./KG 77	Do 17 Z				Operational
3.7.1940	2./KG 77	Do 17 Z				Operational
3.7.1940	7./KG 77	Do 17 Z				Operational
3.7.1940	8./KG 77	Do 17 Z	2642		3Z+GS	Operational
3.7.1940	8./KG 77	Do 17 Z				Operational
3.7.1940	9./KG 77	Do 17 Z				Operational
4.7.1940	6./KG 2	Do 17 Z				Operational
4.7.1940	Stab II/KG 2	Do 17 Z				Operational
4.7.1940	4./KG 77	Do 17 Z				Operational
5.7.1940	5.(F)/122	Do 17 P				Non-operational
6.7.1940	1.(F)/120	Do 17 P			A6+JH	Operational
6.7.1940	III/KG 3	Do 17 Z				Non-operational
7.7.1940	2.(F)/11	Do 17 P-1			6M+AK	Non-operational
7.7.1940	4.(F)/121	Do 17 P			7A+FM	Operational
7.7.1940	2.(F)/123	Do 17 P			4U+KK	Operational
7.7.1940	2.(F)/123	Do 17 P			4U+FK	Operational

DORNIER Do 17 AIRCRAFT CASUALTIES

Country	Location	Details
United Kingdom	Jersey	Aborted take off. Damage 40%.
France	Marquise, 12 km NE Boulogne-sur-Mer	Force-landed after combat with 610 Squadron. Damage 90%.
United Kingdom	Withernsea	Shot down into North Sea by 616 Squadron. Total loss.
United Kingdom	Harwich, 16 km SE Ipswich	Combat with 56 Squadron. Total loss.
United Kingdom	(Margate)	Combat, probably with 54 Squadron. Total loss.
United Kingdom	Near Brighton	Combat with 43 Squadron. Damage ?%.
United Kingdom	Baybrooks, Horsmonden, 12 km SE Tonbridge, Kent	Force-landed following combat with 32 Squadron. Total loss.
France	NW Condette, 8 km S Boulogne-sur-Mer	Hit ground in bad weather. Total loss.
France	Near Boulogne-sur-Mer	Force-landed probably following combat with 610 Squadron. Total loss.
France	Channel coast	Damaged in combat with 79 Squadron. Damage ?%.
France	Saint-Omer	Damaged in action with 79 Squadron. Damage 40%.
France	Near Vrécourt, 43 km ENE Chaumont	Total loss.
France	Thury	Landing accident. Damage 5%.
Sweden	Sangis	Force-landed during transfer flight due to bad weather. Total loss.
		Premature bomb detonation. Damage 95%.
France	6 km WNW Rouen	Probably technical accident. Total loss.
France	Near Rouen	Engine failure following combat. Damage 60%.
United Kingdom	Channel	Shot down by either 145 Squadron or 601 Squadron. Total loss.
United Kingdom	Channel	Shot down by either 145 Squadron or 601 Squadron. Total loss.

DORNIER Do 17 IN THE BATTLE OF BRITAIN

Date	Unit	Type	W/NR	SKZ	Codes	Duty
7.7.1940	4./KG 2	Do 17 Z				Operational
7.7.1940	I/KG 76	Do 17 Z				Non-operational
8.7.1940	III/KG 2	Do 17 Z				Operational
8.7.1940	5./KG 3	Do 17 Z				Enemy action
9.7.1940	4./KG 3	Do 17 Z-2				Operational
9.7.1940	Stabsst./KG 76	Do 17 Z			F1+BA	Non-operational
10.7.1940	2.(F)/11	Do 17 P-1				Non-operational
10.7.1940	4.(F)/121	Do 17 P-1				Operational
10.7.1940	1./KG 2	Do 17 Z				Operational
10.7.1940	2./KG 2	Do 17 Z				Operational
10.7.1940	2./KG 2	Do 17 Z				Operational
10.7.1940	3./KG 2	Do 17 Z			U5+HL	Operational
10.7.1940	3./KG 2	Do 17 Z			U5+FL	Operational
10.7.1940	4./KG 3	Do 17 Z				Operational
11.7.1940	2.(F)/11	Do 17 P-1				Operational
11.7.1940	4./KG 2	Do 17 Z	2542		U5+GM	Operational
11.7.1940	1./KG 3	Do 17 Z				Operational
11.7.1940	Wekusta 26	Do 17				Operational
12.7.1940	5./KG 2	Do 17 Z				Operational
12.7.1940	5./KG 2	Do 17 Z				Operational
13.7.1940	4.(F)/14	Do 17 M				Operational
13.7.1940	2.(F)/123	Do 17 P			4U+DK	Operational
16.7.1940	5.(F)/122	Do 17 P				Operational
16.7.1940	Stabsst./KG 2	Do 17 Z				Operational

DORNIER Do 17 AIRCRAFT CASUALTIES

Country	Location	Details
France	10 km N Boulogne-sur-Mer	Force-landed following combat. Damage 80%.
France	Beauvais	Landing accident. Damage 10%.
France	Saint-Omer	Force-landed following combat possibly with 610 Squadron. Damage 50%.
France	Airfield – Laon-Chambry	Air attack. Damage 5%.
Belgium	Near Antwerp	Force-landed after combat. Total loss.
France	Airfield – Etaples-Le Touquet	Force-landed after combat, possibly with 610 Squadron. Damage 40%.
France	Airfield – Cherbourg	Landing accident. Damage 30%.
France	Near Boulogne	Crash-landed following combat, possibly with 145 Squadron. Damage 60%.
France	Near Marquise, 12 km NE Boulogne-sur-Mer	Force-landed following combat. Damage 70%.
United Kingdom	Channel SE Dungeness	Crashed following combat with 111 Squadron. Total loss.
United Kingdom	Near Dover	Fighter action. Damage ?%.
	Near Dover	Fighter action. Total loss.
United Kingdom	Dungeness Roads Buoy, Kent	Crashed in sea following collision with Hurricane of 111 Squadron. Total loss.
United Kingdom	Winterton	Shot down by 66 Squadron. Total loss.
United Kingdom	Sea Portsmouth - Poole	Probably shot down by 601 Squadron. Total loss.
France	Saint-Léger	Crash-landed following combat with 85 Squadron. Damage 50%.
United Kingdom	English E.coast	Damaged in combat with 66 Squadron and 242 Squadron.
	Sea	Unknown. Total loss.
United Kingdom	North Sea	Crashed following combat with 17 Squadron. Total loss.
United Kingdom	North Sea	Crashed following combat with 17 Squadron. Total loss.
France	Near Caen	Force-landed following combat. Damage 10%.
United Kingdom	Near Chesil Beach, Dorset	Shot down by 238 Squadron. Total loss.
France	Haute Fontaine	Landing accident. Damage 40%.
France	Saint-Inglevert, 11 km SW Calais	Landing accident following combat.

DORNIER Do 17 IN THE BATTLE OF BRITAIN

Date	Unit	Type	W/NR	SKZ	Codes	Duty
16.7.1940	II/KG 3	Do 17 Z				Non-operational
18.7.1940	Stabsst./St.G 77	Do 17 M				Operational
19.7.1940	4.(F)/121	Do 17 P	1098		7A+CM	Operational
20.7.1940	1.(F)/120	Do 17 P-1			A6+HH	Operational
20.7.1940	5.(F)/122	Do 17 P				Operational
20.7.1940	9./KG 2	Do 17 Z				Operational
20.7.1940	Stabsst./St.G 2	Do 17 M				Operational
21.7.1940	4.(F)/14	Do 17 M			5F+OM	Operational
22.7.1940	4.(F)/121	Do 17 P	3598		7A+DM	Operational
22.7.1940	Stabsst./St.G 1	Do 17 M				Operational
23.7.1940	1./Kü.Fl.Gr. 606	Do 17 Z-3	3487		7T+BH	Operational
23.7.1940	2./KG 3	Do 17 Z				Operational
24.7.1940	5./KG 2	Do 17 Z				Operational
24.7.1940	5./KG 2	Do 17 Z				Operational
25.7.1940	Stabsst./St.G 1	Do 17 M			A5+EA	Operational
26.7.1940	4./KG 3	Do 17 Z-3				Operational
26.7.1940	Stab KG 3	Do 17 Z-3				Operational
26.7.1940	3./KG 76	Do 17 Z				Operational
26.7.1940	8./KG 76	Do 17 Z				Operational
27.7.1940	5.(F)/122	Do 17 P				Operational
29.7.1940	Stabsst./KG 2	Do 17 Z				Operational
29.7.1940	Stab III/KG 76	Do 17 Z				Operational
30.7.1940	2./KG 76	Do 17 Z			F1+AK	Non-operational
2.8.1940	8./KG 2	Do 17 Z				Operational
2.8.1940	8./KG 2	Do 17 Z				Operational
2.8.1940	5./NJG 1	Do 17 Z				Operational

DORNIER Do 17 AIRCRAFT CASUALTIES

Country	Location	Details
Belgium	Sint-Niklaas, 19 km SW Antwerp	Landing accident. Damage 15%.
United Kingdom	Channel	Unknown. Total loss.
United Kingdom	Channel near Brighton	Shot down by 145 Squadron. Total loss.
United Kingdom	50 km E. Aberdeen	Shot down by 603 Squadron. Total loss.
France	Rouen	Landing accident due to engine failure. Damage 6%.
Belgium	Zuyenkerke	Force-landed following combat. Damage 80%.
France	200m NE Airfield – Théville	Crashed following engine failure. Total loss.
United Kingdom	Nutford Farm, Blandford, Dorset	Shot down by 238 Squadron. Total loss.
United Kingdom	Channel, 32 km Selsey, Sussex	Shot down by 145 Squadron. Total loss.
France	Airfield – Ouilly-le-Tesson	Burst tyre following engine failure. Damage 30%.
United Kingdom	100 km E. Aberdeen	Shot down by 603 Squadron. Total loss.
United Kingdom	50 km E.Lowestoft, 34 km SE. Norwich	Possibly shot down by 242 Squadron. Total loss.
United Kingdom	North Foreland	Combat with 64 Squadron. Damage 5%.
United Kingdom	North Foreland	Combat with 64 Squadron and 65 Squadron. Damage 50%.
United Kingdom	East Fleet Farm, Fleet, Dorset	Shot down by 152 Squadron. Total loss.
Belgium	3 km NE Gembloux, 15 km NW Namur	Crashed following fuel shortage Total loss.
Belgium	Antwerp	Landing accident. Damage 10%.
United Kingdom	Target Southend	Unknown. Total loss.
France	Airfield – Cormeilles-en-Vexin	Take off accident. Damage 30%.
France	Haute Fontaine	Fighter action. Damage 5%.
France	Airfield – Saint-Inglevert	Damaged in combat with 610 Squadron. Damage 60%.
United Kingdom	Channel	Apparently rammed by Spitfire. Damage ?%.
France	Noailles (near Airfield – La Boessie?)	Total loss.
France	Airfield – Campagne-lès-Guînes	Landing accident. Damage 20%.
France	Airfield – Campagne-lès-Guînes	Landin accident. Damage 60%.
Holland	Airfield – Amsterdam-Schiphol	Landing accident. Damage 45%.

DORNIER Do 17 IN THE BATTLE OF BRITAIN

Date	Unit	Type	W/NR	SKZ	Codes	Duty
2.8.1940	Stabsst./St.G 3	Do 17 M			V4+FA	Non-operational
3.8.1940	4.(F)/14	Do 17 P				Operational
3.8.1940	1./KG 2	Do 17 Z				Operational
3.8.1940	Stabsst./St.G 3	Do 17 M				Non-operational
5.8.1940	3./KG 3	Do 17 Z				Operational
6.8.1940	7./KG 3	Do 17 Z			5K+AR	Operational
6.8.1940	7./KG 3	Do 17 Z				Non-operational
7.8.1940	1./KG 3	Do 17 Z			5K+LH	Non-operational
9.8.1940	3.(F)/11	Do 17 P-1			6M+GL	Non-operational
11.8.1940	9./KG 2	Do 17 Z				Operational
11.8.1940	9./KG 2	Do 17 Z				Operational
11.8.1940	9./KG 2	Do 17 Z				Operational
12.8.1940	3./KG 2	Do 17 Z				Operational
12.8.1940	4./KG 2	Do 17 Z				Operational
12.8.1940	4./KG 2	Do 17 Z				Operational
12.8.1940	9./KG 2	Do 17 Z				Operational
13.8.1940	3.(F)/22	Do 17 P				Operational
13.8.1940	7./KG 2	Do 17 Z			U5+FR	Operational
13.8.1940	7./KG 2	Do 17 Z				Operational
13.8.1940	7./KG 2	Do 17 Z				Operational
13.8.1940	7./KG 2	Do 17 Z			U5+ER	Operational
13.8.1940	8./KG 2	Do 17 Z			U5+DS	Operational
13.8.1940	8./KG 2	Do 17 Z				Operational
13.8.1940	8./KG 2	Do 17 Z				Operational
13.8.1940	8./KG 2	Do 17 Z				Operational
13.8.1940	8./KG 2	Do 17 Z				Operational
13.8.1940	Stab III/KG 2	Do 17 Z				Operational

DORNIER Do 17 AIRCRAFT CASUALTIES

Country	Location	Details
France	Airfield – Dinard	Crashed in flames due to engine problems. Total loss.
United Kingdom	Channel	Unknown. Total loss.
France	Melovres	Crashed in fog. Total loss.
France	Airfield – Dinard	Crashed after take off due to problems with port engine. Total loss.
Belgium	Airfield – Le Culot	Damaged on landing. Damage 15%.
United Kingdom	30 km E Lowestoft, 34 km SE Norwich	Shot down by 85 Squadron. Total loss.
Belgium	Saint-Trond, 16 km SW Hasselt	Landing accident. Damage 30%.
Belgium	Airfield – Le Culot	Landing accident. Damage 75%.
Norway	Airfield – Oslo-Fornebu	Unknown. Total loss.
France	Off Calais	Fighter action. Damage 8%.
France	Off Calais	Fighter action. Damage 5%.
Belgium	Ostende - Calais	Fighter action. Damage 5%.
France	Saint-Inglevert, 11 km SW Calais	Crashed following damage in combat and then engine failure. Total loss.
France	Saint-Omer	Crash-landed following combats. Total loss.
United Kingdom	Canterbury	Combat. Damage ?%.
United Kingdom	Folkestone	Fighter action. Total loss.
Denmark	Kattegat	Crashed in sea. Total loss.
United Kingdom	Birchington, 19 km NE Canterbury, Kent	Crashed following fighter action. Total loss.
France	Calais	Landing accident after comnbat damage. Damage 20%.
United Kingdom	Thames Estuary	Fighter action. Damage 45%.
United Kingdom	Stodmarsh, 8 km NE Canterbury, Kent	Force-landed following combat. Total loss.
United Kingdom	Seasalter, 9 km NW Canterbury, Kent	Crashed following combat. Total loss.
United Kingdom	Sheerness, 28 km NW Canterbury	Fighter action. Damage ?%.
United Kingdom	Sheerness, 28 km NW Canterbury	Fighter action. Damage 5%.
United Kingdom	Sheerness, 28 km NW Canterbury	Fighter action. Damage ?%.
United Kingdom	Sheerness, 28 km NW Canterbury	Fighter action. Damage 20%.
United Kingdom	Bray-Dunes, 11 km ENE Dumkirk	Crashed following combat. Total loss.

DORNIER Do 17 IN THE BATTLE OF BRITAIN

Date	Unit	Type	W/NR	SKZ	Codes	Duty
13.8.1940	Stabsst. KG 2	Do 17 Z			U5+KA	Operational
13.8.1940	Stabsst. KG 2	Do 17 Z				Operational
15.8.1940	3.(F)/31	Do 17 P				Operational
15.8.1940	2./KG 3	Do 17 Z-2				Operational
15.8.1940	Stab I/KG 3	Do 17 Z-3				Operational
15.8.1940	6./KG 3	Do 17 Z-2			5K+LP	Operational
15.8.1940	6./KG 3	Do 17 Z-2				Operational
15.8.1940	6./KG 3	Do 17 Z-2				Operational
15.8.1940	6./KG 3	Do 17 Z-2				Operational
15.8.1940	6./KG 3	Do 17 Z-2				Operational
15.8.1940	6./KG 3	Do 17 Z-3				Operational
15.8.1940	Stab KG 76	Do 17 Z				Non-operational
15.8.1940	Stabsst./KG 76	Do 17 Z				Operational
16.8.1940	3./KG 2	Do 17 Z-2			U5+LL	Operational
16.8.1940	3./KG 2	Do 17 Z-3			U5+BL	Operational
16.8.1940	3./KG 2	Do 17 Z-3				Operational
16.8.1940	Stab III/KG 76	Do 17 Z-2				Operational
18.8.1940	6./KG 2	Do 17 Z-3				Operational
18.8.1940	1./KG 76	Do 17 Z	2504		F1+IH	Operational
18.8.1940	2./KG 76	Do 17 Z				Operational
18.8.1940	3./KG 76	Do 17 Z				Operational
18.8.1940	III/KG 76	Do 17 Z				Operational
18.8.1940	8./KG 76	Do 17 Z				Operational
18.8.1940	8./KG 76	Do 17 Z-2				Operational
18.8.1940	9./KG 76	Do 17 Z				Operational
18.8.1940	9./KG 76	Do 17 Z				Operational

DORNIER Do 17 AIRCRAFT CASUALTIES

Country	Location	Details
United Kingdom	Pherbec Bridge, Barham, 10 km SE Canterbury, Kent	Shot down by 111 Squadron. Total loss.
United Kingdom	Thames Estuary	Fighter action. Damage 35%.
United Kingdom	S Portland	Probably shot down by 602 Squadron. Total loss.
United Kingdom	Dover	Fighter action. Damage 8%.
France	Wissant	Landing accident after combat damage over Rochester. Damage 60%.
United Kingdom	2 km E Reculver, 14 km NE Canterbury, Kent	Crashed in sea following fighter action. Total loss.
France		Combat damage. Damage 8%.
United Kingdom	Channel between Deal and Ramsgate	Crashed in sea following combat with 111 Squadron. Total loss.
France		Flak. Damage 8%.
France		Combat damage. Damage 8%.
France		Combat damage. Damage 60%.
France	Colonie	Landing accident. Damage 30%.
France	Target Redhill	Damaged by fighter. Damage 5%.
United Kingdom	Summerfield near Staple, 12 km ESE Canterbury, Kent	Crashed following fighter action. Total loss.
France	Calais-Marck	Crashed following fighter action. Total loss.
United Kingdom	Whitstable Beach,10 km NNW Canterbury, Kent	Exploded in the air following fighter action. Total loss.
United Kingdom	Moatlands Farm, Brenchley, 10 km ENE Tunbridge Wells, Kent	Shot down by 111 Squadron. Total loss.
United Kingdom	Thames Estuary	Fighter action. Damage 3%.
United Kingdom	Mill Lane, Hurst Green, Surrey	Crashed following fighter action. Total loss.
France		Fighter action. Damage 20%.
France		Fighter action. Damage 3%.
France	Cormeilles	Fighter action. Damage 10-60%.
United Kingdom	Channel	Crashed following fighter action. Total loss.
France	Calais	Landing accident after combat. Damage 50%.
France	Abbeville	Force-landed after combat. Damage ?%.
United Kingdom	Channel	Force-landed in sea. Total loss.

DORNIER Do 17 IN THE BATTLE OF BRITAIN

Date	Unit	Type	W/NR	SKZ	Codes	Duty
18.8.1940	9./KG 76	Do 17 Z				Operational
18.8.1940	9./KG 76	Do 17 Z				Operational
18.8.1940	9./KG 76	Do 17 Z			F1+JT	Operational
18.8.1940	9./KG 76	Do 17 Z-2			F1+DT	Operational
18.8.1940	9./KG 76	Do 17 Z-2			F1+HT	Operational
18.8.1940	9./KG 76	Do 17 Z-2				Operational
18.8.1940	9./KG 76	Do 17 Z-2				Operational
18.8.1940	9./KG 76	Do 17 Z-2				Operational
18.8.1940	9./KG 76	Do 17 Z-3			F1+CT	Operational
19.8.1940	7./KG 2	Do 17 Z			U5+DR	Operational
20.8.1940	7./KG 2	Do 17 Z-3				Operational
20.8.1940	9./KG 2	Do 17 Z-3				Operational
20.8.1940	9./KG 3	Do 17 Z-3			5K+FT	Operational
21.8.1940	2./KG 2	Do 17 Z-3			U5+FK	Operational
21.8.1940	8./KG 2	Do 17 Z			U5+CS	Operational
21.8.1940	4./KG 3	Do 17 Z-3				Operational
21.8.1940	4./KG 3	Do 17 Z-3				Operational
21.8.1940	6./KG 3	Do 17 Z-2			5K+BP	Operational
21.8.1940	6./KG 3	Do 17 Z-3			5K+AP	Operational
22.8.1940	1./KG 2	Do 17 Z			U5+LH	Non-operational
23.8.1940	Stabsst./KG 2	Do 17 Z			U5+EA	Operational
23.8.1940	7./KG 76	Do 17 Z-2				Operational
25.8.1940	3./KG 76	Do 17 Z				Operational
26.8.1940	1./Kü.Fl.Gr. 606	Do 17 Z-3	2676		7T+GH	Operational

DORNIER Do 17 AIRCRAFT CASUALTIES

Country	Location	Details
France	Amiens	Force-landed following combat. Damage ?%.
France		Force-landed in sea after combat. Total loss.
France	Airfield- Norrent-Fontès	Flak. Damage 5%.
United Kingdom	Leaves Green, 3 km N Biggin Hill, Kent	Force-landed on fire after Flak and fighter damage. Total loss.
United Kingdom	Golf Road, Kenley, Surrey	Crashed on fire due to Flak. Total loss.
United Kingdom	Channel	Ditched after combat. Total loss.
United Kingdom	Channel	Ditched after combat. Total loss.
France	Calais	Force-landed following fighter action. Damage 50%.
France	Near Abbeville	Force-landed following combat. Damage 60%.
United Kingdom	Channel	Crashed in sea. Total loss.
United Kingdom	Aldeburgh, 27 km NE Felixstowe	Fighter action. Damage 25%.
France	Attacked off Orfordness	Damaged in combat with 257 Squadron.
United Kingdom	Capel Hill Farm, Leysdown on Sea, 17 km NW Canterbury	Probably shot down by 615 Squadron.
United Kingdom	Conifer Hill House, Harleston, Suffolk	Shot down by 242 Squadron. Total loss.
United Kingdom	Gippeswyke Park, Ipswich, 25 km NE Colchester, Suffolk	Shot down by 56 Squadron. Total loss.
United Kingdom	North Sea Near Scott Head, Brancaster Roads, Norfolk	Shot down by 611 Squadron. Total loss.
United Kingdom	North Sea Near Skegness, Lincolnshire	Shot down by 611 Squadron. Total loss.
United Kingdom	Bilsby Near Alford, Lincolnshire	Mid-air collision with below. Total loss.
United Kingdom	Farletsthorpe, Alford, Lincolnshire	Mid-air collision with above. Total loss
France	Escaudoeuvres, 3 km NE Cambrai	Crashed on transfer flight. Total loss.
United Kingdom	Spring Wood, Lodge Farm, Wickhambrook, Suffolk	Force-landed with Flak damage. Total loss.
France	Cormeilles	Landing accident. Damage 70%.
United Kingdom	Channel	Crashed in sea following fighter action. Total loss.
United Kingdom	St. George's Channel	Crashed. Total loss.

DORNIER Do 17 IN THE BATTLE OF BRITAIN

Date	Unit	Type	W/NR	SKZ	Codes	Duty
26.8.1940	1./KG 2	Do 17 Z				Operational
26.8.1940	2./KG 2	Do 17 Z				Operational
26.8.1940	2./KG 2	Do 17 Z-3	2425		U5+GK	Operational
26.8.1940	2./KG 2	Do 17 Z-3	2637		U5+LK	Operational
26.8.1940	3./KG 2	Do 17 Z-2				Operational
26.8.1940	4./KG 2	Do 17 Z-2	3445		U5+MM	Operational
26.8.1940	7./KG 2	Do 17 Z-2			U5+TR	Operational
26.8.1940	7./KG 2	Do 17 Z-3	1207		U5+BR	Operational
26.8.1940	7./KG 2	Do 17 Z-3			U5+LR	Operational
26.8.1940	9./KG 2	Do 17 Z				Operational
26.8.1940	2./KG 3	Do 17 Z-2	2541			Operational
26.8.1940	7./KG 3	Do 17 Z	3329		5K+GR	Operational
26.8.1940	7./KG 3	Do 17 Z	3602			Operational
26.8.1940	7./KG 3	Do 17 Z-2	1160		5K+AR	Operational
26.8.1940	7./KG 3	Do 17 Z-3	2646		5K+ER	Operational
26.8.1940	7./KG 3	Do 17 Z-3	2822			Operational
27.8.1940	3.(F)/10	Do 17 P	3545		T1+BL	Operational
27.8.1940	3.(F)/31	Do 17 P			5D+JL	Operational
27.8.1940	5./KG 2	Do 17 Z-2	4188			Operational
27.8.1940	6./KG 2	Do 17 Z-3	2784			Operational
28.8.1940	2./Kü.Fl.Gr. 606	Do 17 Z			7T+DK	Operational
28.8.1940	1./KG 3	Do 17 Z-3	2807		5K+JH	Operational
28.8.1940	3./KG 3	Do 17 Z-2	3378			Operational

DORNIER Do 17 AIRCRAFT CASUALTIES

Country	Location	Details
France		Fighter action. Damage ?%.
United Kingdom	Thameshaven	Fighter action. Damage ?%.
United Kingdom	3 km SW Eastchurch, 20 km NW Canterbury, Kent	Force-landed following combat probably with 85 Squadron. Total loss.
United Kingdom	Airfield – Rochford	Force-landed following combat. Total loss.
United Kingdom	Near London	Combat damage. Damage 15-60%.
Belgium	Near Namur	Crashed following fighter action. Total loss.
United Kingdom	Cole End, Saffron Walden, Essex	Crashed following fighter action. Total loss.
United Kingdom	Whepstead Near Bury St. Edmunds, 39 km E Cambridge	Force-landed following fighter action. Total loss.
United Kingdom	Higham's Farm, Thaxted, 32 km SE Cambridge, Essex	Crashed on fire after combat. Total loss.
United Kingdom	Near Colchester	Fighter action. Damage ?%.
Belgium	Near Tirlemont, 17 km SE Louvain	Force-landed following fuel shortage Damage 80%.
France	Channel	Shot down in combat with 264 Squadron. Total loss.
France	Calais-Marck	Force-landed following combat with 264 Squadron. Total loss.
United Kingdom	Goodwin Sands, Kent	Force-landed following combat with 264 Squadron. Total loss.
United Kingdom	Foreness Point, Isle of Thanet, Kent	Force-landed following combat with 264 Squadron. Total loss.
France	Saint-Merville	Force-landed following fuel shortage Damage 10-60%.
France	Cap Gris-Nez	Shot down by 56 Squadron. Total loss.
United Kingdom	Hardwick Farm, Tavistock, Devon	Force-landed following combat with 238 Squadron. Total loss.
Belgium	Near Slijpe	Damaged by nightfighter. Crew baled out. Total loss.
France	Near Saint-André	Crash-landed following fuel shortage. Damage 35%.
France	2 km from Hennebont	Combat. Damage ?%.
Belgium	Chêne Al Pierre, 27 km NE Marche-en-Famenne	Unknown. Total loss.
Belgium	Rocherath, 19 km E Malmedy	Crashed and burned out. Total loss.

DORNIER Do 17 IN THE BATTLE OF BRITAIN

Date	Unit	Type	W/NR	SKZ	Codes	Duty
28.8.1940	4./KG 3	Do 17 Z-2	3225			Operational
28.8.1940	6./KG 3	Do 17 Z	3411		5K+DP	Operational
28.8.1940	6./KG 3	Do 17 Z-3	4251		5K+LP	Operational
29.8.1940	1./Kü.Fl.Gr. 606	Do 17 Z-3	2878		7T+GH	Operational
29.8.1940	6./KG 2	Do 17 Z-3	2839		U5+FP	Operational
29.8.1940	6./KG 3	Do 17 Z-3	3480		5K+FP	Non-operationa
30.8.1940	3.(F)/22	Do 17 P	1119		4N+AL	Operational
30.8.1940	3./Kü.Fl.Gr. 606	Do 17 Z-3	2838		7T+GL	Operational
30.8.1940	9./KG 2	Do 17 Z-3	2868		U5+FT	Operational
31.8.1940	5./KG 2	Do 17 Z-3	3483		U5+CN	Operational
31.8.1940	8./KG 2	Do 17 Z				Operational
31.8.1940	Stab III/KG 2	Do 17 Z-2	3356	BG+NR	U5+AD	Operational
31.8.1940	3./KG 3	Do 17 Z-2	1178		5K+KL	Operational
31.8.1940	3./KG 3	Do 17 Z-2	3299		5K+HL	Operational
31.8.1940	4./KG 3	Do 17 Z				Operational
31.8.1940	4./KG 3	Do 17 Z				Operational
31.8.1940	4./KG 3	Do 17 Z-2	3264		5K+KM	Operational
31.8.1940	4./KG 3	Do 17 Z-2	3456		5K+BC	Operational
31.8.1940	4./KG 3	Do 17 Z-3	2669		5K+LM	Operational
31.8.1940	4./KG 3	Do 17 Z-3	3458		5K+EM	Operational
31.8.1940	5./KG 3	Do 17 Z-3	3414		5K+GN	Operational
31.8.1940	2./KG 76	Do 17 Z	3316		F1+BK	Operational
1.9.1940	2./KG 76	Do 17 Z				Operational
1.9.1940	2./KG 76	Do 17 Z				Operational
1.9.1940	9./KG 76	Do 17 Z	3369		F1+AT	Operational
1.9.1940	9./KG 76	Do 17 Z				Operational
1.9.1940	9./KG 76	Do 17 Z				Operational
2.9.1940	8./KG 3	Do 17 Z-2	1145		5K+MS	Operational

DORNIER Do 17 AIRCRAFT CASUALTIES

Country	Location	Details
France		Fighter action. Total loss.
France	Mardyck, 9 km WSW Dunkirk	Combat with fighter. Damage 3%.
United Kingdom	Near Foreness Point, Isle of Thanet, Kent	Ditched after combat with 54 Squadron. Total loss.
United Kingdom	North Sea	Force-landed. Total loss.
France	Near Persan	Nightfighter. Damage 80%.
Belgium	Doomkerke, 26 km W.Gent	Collided with radio mast, crashed and caught fire. Total loss.
United Kingdom	North Sea	Unknown. Total loss.
Spain	Güeñes, 12 km SW Bilbao	Force-landed after getting lost in fog. Total loss.
Belgium	Near Brügge	Crashed due to the pilot getting into a spin in cloud. Total loss.
United Kingdom	Duxford	Fighter action. Total loss.
United Kingdom	Colchester	Fighter action. Damage ?%.
United Kingdom	Colchester	Fighter action. Damage 5%.
France	Saint-Omer	Fighter action. Total loss.
France	Merville	Landing accident. Damage 10-60%.
United Kingdom	Hornchurch	Fighter action. Damage ?%.
France		Flak. Damage ?%.
United Kingdom	Eastwick Farm, Burnham-on-Crouch, Essex	Force-landed following fighter action. Total loss.
United Kingdom	Hornchurch	Flak. Damage 12%.
United Kingdom	Sandwich, Kent	Force-landed following combat. Total loss.
United Kingdom	Hornchurch	Combat damage. Damage 8%.
United Kingdom	Near Goodwin Sands	Force-landed in sea following fighter action. Total loss.
United Kingdom	Newchurch near Dungeness, Kent	Shot down by 72 Squadron. Total loss.
France		Flak. Damage ?%.
France		Unknown. Damage ?%.
United Kingdom	Tarts Field, Lydd Kent	Shot down by 85 Squadron. Total loss.
United Kingdom	Tonbridge area	Flak. Damage ?%.
France		Unknown. Damage ?%.
Belgium	Le Culot	Combat. Damage ?%.

DORNIER Do 17 IN THE BATTLE OF BRITAIN

Date	Unit	Type	W/NR	SKZ	Codes	Duty
2.9.1940	9./KG 3	Do 17 Z-2	1187		5K+MT	Operational
2.9.1940	9./KG 3	Do 17 Z-2	3269		5K+BT	Operational
2.9.1940	9./KG 3	Do 17 Z-3	3390		5K+GT	Operational
3.9.1940	5./KG 2	Do 17 Z-2	3450		U5+AN	Operational
5.9.1940	6./KG 2	Do 17 Z	2828		U5+KP	Operational
5.9.1940	6./KG 2	Do 17 Z-2	1134		U5+FP	Operational
5.9.1940	8./KG 3	Do 17 Z-2	1145		5K+MS	Operational
7.9.1940	4./KG 2	Do 17 Z	2830		U5+FM	Operational
7.9.1940	9./KG 2	Do 17 Z				Operational
7.9.1940	Stabsst./KG 2	Do 17 Z	2674		U5+CA	Operational
7.9.1940	5./KG 3	Do 17 Z	2840		5K+FN	Operational
7.9.1940	III/KG 3	Do 17 Z				Operational
7.9.1940	8./KG 3	Do 17 Z				Operational
7.9.1940	8./KG 3	Do 17 Z				Operational
7.9.1940	9./KG 3	Do 17 Z				Operational
7.9.1940	Stabsst./KG 3	Do 17 Z-3	2619		5K+DA	Operational
7.9.1940	Stabsst./KG 76	Do 17 Z	2596		F1+BA	Operational
8.9.1940	5./KG 2	Do 17 Z	3415		U5+LN	Operational
8.9.1940	5./KG 2	Do 17 Z			U5+DN	Operational
8.9.1940	5./KG 2	Do 17 Z-2	1130		U5+FN	Operational
8.9.1940	5./KG 2	Do 17 Z-3	2668		U5+BN	Operational
8.9.1940	6./KG 2	Do 17 Z	2785		U5+CP	Operational
8.9.1940	3./KG 3	Do 17 Z-2	3321		5K+CL	Operational
8.9.1940	3./KG 3	Do 17 Z-2	3436		5K+GL	Operational
9.9.1940	Stab./ KG 2	Do 17 Z	2674		U5+CA	Operational
10.9.1940	9./KG 76	Do 17 Z-3	2778		F1+ET	Operational

DORNIER Do 17 AIRCRAFT CASUALTIES

Country	Location	Details
Belgium	Saint-Trond	Landing accident after combat. Total loss.
United Kingdom	Airfield – Rochford, Essex	Force-landed following fighter action. Total loss.
France	Saint-Omer	Crash-landed. Damage 65%.
United Kingdom	Lodge Farm Near Pyefleet Creek, Langenhoe, Essex	Shot down by 17 Squadron. Total loss.
France	Near Saint-Omer	Probably damaged in combat with 41 Squadron and force-landed. Damage 20%.
France	Near Calais	Probably damaged in combat with 41 Squadron and force-landed. Damage 20%.
Belgium	Le Culot	Landing accident. Damage 33%.
United Kingdom	Near London	Crashed on return after combat. Total loss.
United Kingdom	London area	Flak. Damage ?%.
United Kingdom	London area	Fighter action. Damage 10%.
France	Calais	Force-landed after combat. Damage 50%.
France		Fighter action. Damage ?%.
United Kingdom	London	Flak. Damage ?%.
United Kingdom	London	Flak. Damage ?%.
France		Combat. Damage ?%.
United Kingdom	London	Flak. Total loss.
United Kingdom	Sundridge, 2 km west of Sevenoaks, Kent	Collided with Spitfire of 234 Squadron. Total loss.
United Kingdom	Leeds Near Maidstone, Kent	Hit by Flak and exploded. Total loss.
United Kingdom	London area	Engine failure after Flak damage. Damage ?%.
United Kingdom	Farningham Road Railway Station, London, Kent	Hit by Flak and exploded. Total loss.
United Kingdom	Near Farningham Road Railway Station, London, Kent	Hit by Flak and exploded. Total loss.
United Kingdom	London area	Rammed by RAF fighter. Damage 35%.
Belgium	Ertvelde, 14 km N Gent	Mid-air collision with below. Total loss.
Belgium	Ertvelde, 14 km N Gent	Mid-air collision with above. Damage 60%.
United Kingdom	Near London	Fighter action. Damage 30%.
United Kingdom	Lower Sheriff Cottage, West Hoathly, 10 km SE Crawley	Shot down in combat with 72 Squadron and 92 Squadron. Total loss.

DORNIER Do 17 IN THE BATTLE OF BRITAIN

Date	Unit	Type	W/NR	SKZ	Codes	Duty
14.9.1940	2.(F)/22	Do 17 P	3519		4N+CK	Operational
14.9.1940	1./Kü.Fl.Gr. 606	Do 17 Z-2	1213		7T+BH	Operational
14.9.1940	1./Kü.Fl.Gr. 606	Do 17 Z-3	1216		7T+FH	Operational
14.9.1940	1./Kü.Fl.Gr. 606	Do 17 Z-3	2815		7T+NH	Operational
14.9.1940	2./Kü.Fl.Gr. 606	Do 17 Z	2687		7T+FK	Operational
15.9.1940	5./KG 2	Do 17 Z				Operational
15.9.1940	5./KG 2	Do 17 Z-2	1135		U5+MN	Operational
15.9.1940	5./KG 2	Do 17 Z-3	2304		U5+HN	Operational
15.9.1940	5./KG 2	Do 17 Z-3	2678		U5+CN	Operational
15.9.1940	7./KG 2	Do 17 Z	2539		U5+ER	Operational
15.9.1940	7./KG 2	Do 17 Z-2	1153		U5+KR	Operational
15.9.1940	8./KG 2	Do 17 Z	2549		U5+FS	Operational
15.9.1940	8./KG 2	Do 17 Z	3401		U5+DS	Operational
15.9.1940	8./KG 2	Do 17 Z	3432		U5+JS	Operational
15.9.1940	8./KG 2	Do 17 Z	3440		U5+PS	Operational
15.9.1940	8./KG 2	Do 17 Z-3	2644			Operational
15.9.1940	8./KG 2	Do 17 Z-3	4242		U5+JR	Operational
15.9.1940	8./KG 2	Do 17 Z-3	4245		U5+GS	Operational
15.9.1940	9./KG 2	Do 17 Z	3405		U5+FT	Operational
15.9.1940	9./KG 2	Do 17 Z-2	3230		U5+ET	Operational
15.9.1940	Stabsst./KG 2	Do 17 Z				Operational
15.9.1940	4./KG 3	Do 17 Z-2	3294		5K+DM	Operational
15.9.1940	4./KG 3	Do 17 Z-2	3457		5K+JM	Operational
15.9.1940	4./KG 3	Do 17 Z-3	2879		5K+AM	Operational
15.9.1940	4./KG 3	Do 17 Z-3	2881		5K+CM	Operational
15.9.1940	5./KG 3	Do 17 Z-2	1176		5K+DN	Operational

DORNIER Do 17 AIRCRAFT CASUALTIES

Country	Location	Details
Norway	Airfield – Stavanger-Sola	Burst tyre. Damage 70%.
France	Airfield – Cherbourg-West	Landing accident. Damage 15%.
France	Airfield – Cherbourg-West	Landing accident. Damage 80%.
France	Airfield – Cherbourg-West	Landing accident. Damage 50%.
France	Airfield – Cherbourg-West	Landing accident. Total loss.
United Kingdom	Channel	Fighter action. Damage ?%.
United Kingdom	Channel	Fighter action. Damage 7%.
United Kingdom	Channel off Dungeness	Shot down by Flak and fighters. Total loss.
United Kingdom	Eighteen Pounder Farm, Westfield Near Hastings, East Sussex	Force-landed following combat. Total loss.
United Kingdom	London	Fighter action. Damage 5%.
United Kingdom	Channel	Fighter action. Damage 2%.
United Kingdom	Channel	Fighter action. Total loss.
France	20 km SW Boulogne-sur-Mer	Shot down by 41 Squadron and 249 Squadron. Total loss.
United Kingdom	Channel	Fighter action. Damage 2%.
United Kingdom	The Chase, City Way, Chatham, Kent	Damaged by 73 Squadron and finally shot down by Flak. Total loss
France	Berck	Damaged by fighters and crash-landed. Damage 100%.
France	Near Cambrai	Landing accident. Damage 65%.
United Kingdom	Channel	Fighter action. Total loss.
United Kingdom	Channel Near Herne Bay	Shot down by 46 Squadron. Total loss.
United Kingdom	Nine Acre Wood, Kilndown Near Goudhurst, Kent	Crashed with burning engine after combat. Total loss.
United Kingdom	Channel	Fighter action. Damage ?%.
United Kingdom	Gladstone Road, Laindon Hills, Billericay, Essex	Shot down by 249 Squadron and 504 Squadron. Total loss.
United Kingdom	Perry Street Near Barnehurst Golf Course Near Bexley, Kent	Damage by Flak and finally shot down by 504 Squadron. Total loss.
France	Mardyck	Crash-landed following fighter action. Damage 40%.
United Kingdom	Allhallows, Isle of Grain, Kent	Shot down by 19 Squadron and 310 Squadron. Total loss.
United Kingdom	Thames Estuary	Possibly shot down by 249 Squadron. Total loss.

DORNIER Do 17 IN THE BATTLE OF BRITAIN

Date	Unit	Type	W/NR	SKZ	Codes	Duty
15.9.1940	5./KG 3	Do 17 Z-2	4200		5K+JN	Operational
15.9.1940	5./KG 3	Do 17 Z-3	2649		5K+HN	Operational
15.9.1940	5./KG 3	Do 17 Z-3	3458		5K+GN	Operational
15.9.1940	6./KG 3	Do 17 Z-2	3470	RI+KA	5K+CP	Operational
15.9.1940	6./KG 3	Do 17 Z-3	4237		5K+EM	Operational
15.9.1940	1./KG 76	Do 17 Z	2361		F1+FH	Operational
15.9.1940	1./KG 76	Do 17 Z	2364		F1+EH	Operational
15.9.1940	2./KG 76	Do 17 Z-2	2524		F1+JK	Operational
15.9.1940	3./KG 76	Do 17 Z-3	2651		F1+FL	Operational
15.9.1940	8./KG 76	Do 17 Z	2555		F1+FS	Operational
15.9.1940	8./KG 76	Do 17 Z-2	2578		F1+BS	Operational
15.9.1940	9./KG 76	Do 17 Z	2814		F1+AT	Operational
15.9.1940	9./KG 76	Do 17 Z-2	3322		F1+DT	Operational
18.9.1940	3.(F)/10	Do 17 P	1063		T1+EL	Operational
18.9.1940	3.(F)/10	Do 17 P	1105	PB+MB	T1+HL	Operational
19.9.1940	2./KG 3	Do 17 Z-2	3429		5K+LK	Operational
19.9.1940	6./KG 3	Do 17 Z-2	2535		5K+BP	Operational
19.9.1940	9./KG 3	Do 17 Z-3	2647		5K+GT	Non-operational
20.9.1940	4.(F)/121	Do 17 P	1102			Operational
20.9.1940	3./Kü.Fl.Gr. 606	Do 17 Z-3	1211		7T+ML	Operational
21.9.1940	1./Kü.Fl.Gr. 606	Do 17 Z	3497		7T+LH	Operational
21.9.1940	3./Kü.Fl.Gr. 606	Do 17 Z	3471		7T+CL	Operational
21.9.1940	5./KG 2	Do 17 Z-2	3454		U5+FN	Non-operational

DORNIER Do 17 AIRCRAFT CASUALTIES

Country	Location	Details
United Kingdom	Skinners Farm, Beltring, Kent	Collided with Hurricane of 605 Squadron. Total loss.
France	Calais	Landing accident after fighter action. Damage 3%.
United Kingdom	Wilden Wood, Marden, Kent	Collided with Hurricane of 607 Squadron. Total loss.
United Kingdom	London	Fighter action. Damage 50%.
United Kingdom	London	Fighter action. Damage 15%.
United Kingdom	Victoria Station, London	Crashed after being attacked by Nos. 257, 302, 310, 504 and 609 Squadrons. Total loss.
France	Boulogne-sur-Mer	Force-landed after combat. Damage 60%.
France	Near Poix	Force-landed after combat. Damage 60%.
United Kingdom	Alcroft Farm, Sturry, 4 km NE Canterbury, Kent	Crashed after combat with Nos. 66, 249 and 611 Squadrons. Total loss.
United Kingdom	Lullingstone Castle Farm, Lullingstone, Kent	Crash-landed after combat with Nos. 19, 46, 257, 504 and 609 Squadrons. Total loss.
United Kingdom	Channel 7 km NW Herne Bay	Crashed in sea after finally being shot down by 253 Squadron. Total loss.
United Kingdom	Argos Hill, Rotherfield, East Sussex	Crashed after combat with Nos. 46, 229, 310 and 504 Squadrons. Total loss.
United Kingdom	Underriver, 3 km SE Sevenoaks	Force-landed after combat with Nos. 19, 46, 72, 242, 257 and 605 Squadrons. Total loss.
United Kingdom	Near Dover	Combat with fighters. Damage 12%,
United Kingdom	Appledore	Combat with fighters. Damage 30%.
Belgium	Tessenderlo, 9 km NNE Diest	Force-landed. Damage 30%.
Holland	Dreibrubben	Force-landed following engine failure. Damage 50%.
France	Saint-Albert	Landing accident. Damage 50%.
France	Airfield – Caen-Carpiquet	Fighter action. Damage 60%.
France	Airfield – Quimper	Force-landed following fuel shortage. Damage 80%.
France	Sizun	Force-landed after combat possibly with 79 Squadron. Total loss.
France	4 km S Landernau (Lanvéoc)	Crashed in flames after mid-air collision. Total loss.
France	Saint-Léger	Landing accident. Damage 80%.

DORNIER Do 17 IN THE BATTLE OF BRITAIN

Date	Unit	Type	W/NR	SKZ	Codes	Duty
22.9.1940	7./KG 2	Do 17 Z-3	2858		U5+FR	Operational
22.9.1940	8./KG 76	Do 17 Z-2	2809		F1+HS	Operational
24.9.1940	1./KG 3	Do 17 Z-3	2633		5K+JH	Operational
24.9.1940	1./KG 76	Do 17 Z-2	1184	SG+CO	F1+BH	Operational
24.9.1940	2./KG 76	Do 17 Z	3317		F1+GK	Operational
25.9.1940	7./KG 76	Do 17 Z	4199		F1+ER	Operational
26.9.1940	Stabsst./KG 3	Do 17 Z-3	2591		5K+FA	Operational
27.9.1940	8./KG 2	Do 17 Z	2871		U5+ES	Non-operational
28.9.1940	4./KG 2	Do 17 Z				Operational
28.9.1940	5./KG 2	Do 17 Z	3355		U5+AN	Operational
29.9.1940	4.(F)/14	Do 17 P	1096			Operational
30.9.1940	4./KG 2	Do 17 Z-2	3420	CN+CT	U5+EM	Operational
30.9.1940	8./KG 2	Do 17 Z	2861		U5+BS	Operational
30.9.1940	7./KG 3	Do 17 Z-3	2822		5K+GR	Operational
30.9.1940	8./KG 3	Do 17 Z-3	4227		5K+HR	Operational
30.9.1940	Stab III/KG 3	Do 17 Z-2	3360		5K+AD	Operational
1.10.1940	1./KG 2	Do 17 Z-2	1177		U5+BH	Non-operational
2.10.1940	4./KG 2	Do 17 Z-3	2659		U5+DM	Operational
2.10.1940	Stabsst./KG 2	Do 17 Z	3423		U5+FA	Operational
2.10.1940	9./KG 3	Do 17 Z-2	3270		5K+CT	Operational
3.10.1940	Kü.Fl.Gr. 606	Do 17 Z	2530			Operational
3.10.1940	3./Kü.Fl.Gr. 606	Do 17 Z	3491		7T+EL	Operational
3.10.1940	1./KG 2	Do 17 Z-2	2579		U5+DH	Operational
3.10.1940	2./KG 2	Do 17 Z-3	2638		U5+AK	Operational
3.10.1940	Wekusta 1 Ob.d.L.	Do 17 Z-2	2547		T5+IU	Operational
4.10.1940	1./Kü.Fl.Gr. 606	Do 17 Z				Operational
4.10.1940	1./Kü.Fl.Gr. 606	Do 17 Z-3	3617		7T+CH	Operational
4.10.1940	1./KG 2	Do 17 Z-2	1212		U5+GH	Operational

DORNIER Do 17 AIRCRAFT CASUALTIES

Country	Location	Details
France	Near Cambrai	Landing accident. Damage 65%.
France	Airfield – Clermont	Landing accident. Damage 3%.
Belgium	Airfield – Antwerp-Deurne	Force-landed following fighter action. Damage 60%.
France	Beauvais	Force-landed. Damage 30%.
France	Near Boulogne-sur-Mer	Force-landed after combat with 605 Squadron. Total loss.
France	Near Villers	Force-landed. Damage 12%.
Holland	Near Maastricht	Force-landed after getting lost. Total loss.
France	Masnières, 5 km S Cambrai	Crashed. Total loss.
United Kingdom	Channel	Engine fire after being hit by Flak. Damage ?%.
France	10 km E Airfield – Saint-Léger	Crashed after take off. Total loss.
France	Cresserons near Plumetot	Crashed after take off. Total loss.
France	Near Orléans	Landing accident. Damage 15%.
France	W Bertincourt, 20 km SW Cambrai	Crashed. Total loss.
France	Boulogne-sur-Mer	Force-landed. Damage 70%.
United Kingdom	Channel	Fighter action. Total loss.
France	Saint-Omer	Force-landed. Damage 50%.
France	Mons-en-Chaussée, 21 km WNW Saint-Quentin	Crashed. Total loss.
France	Near Paris	Friendly fire. Total loss.
United Kingdom	Rookery Farm, Cretingham, Suffolk	Shot down by 17 Squadron. Total loss.
Belgium	Le Culot	Crashed. Total loss.
France	Airfield- Brest-Süd	Landing accident. Damage 20%.
United Kingdom	Off Cornwall	Crashed in sea. Total loss.
France	Bapaume, 21 km ESE Arras	Became lost and crash-landed after crew baled out. Damage 40%.
France	NW Marquise	Hit the ground. Damage 95%.
	SE Shetland Isles	Combat with 248 Squadron. Damage not recorded.
United Kingdom	Penrose	Flak. Damage ?%.
France	Caen-Carpiquet	Flak. Total loss.
Germany	Krefeld	Crashed following getting lost. Total loss.

131

DORNIER Do 17 IN THE BATTLE OF BRITAIN

Date	Unit	Type	W/NR	SKZ	Codes	Duty
4.10.1940	6./KG 2	Do 17 Z	4201		U5+EP	Operational
4.10.1940	5./KG 3	Do 17 Z-2	3343		5K+KN	Operational
4.10.1940	III/KG 76	Do 17 Z	2887	PF+EB		Operational
4.10.1940	7./KG 76	Do 17 Z-2	1136	RP+AY	F1+KR	Operational
4.10.1940	9./KG 76	Do 17 Z	2888		F1+DT	Non-operational
4.10.1940	Stabsst./KG 76	Do 17 Z	2610			Operational
4.10.1940	Stabsst./St.G 3	Do 17 Z	2832			Non-operational
6.10.1940	2./KG 3	Do 17 Z-2	2537		5K+AK	Operational
6.10.1940	7./KG 76	Do 17 Z-3	4221		F1+FR	Operational
7.10.1940	4.(F)/11	Do 17 P-1	3527		6M+HM	Non-operational
7.10.1940	Stab St.G 3	Do 17 Z-3	2877			Non-operational
8.10.1940	2.(F)/22	Do 17 P	3576		4N+GK	Operational
9.10.1940	3./Kü.Fl.Gr. 606	Do 17 Z-3	2771		7T+HL	Operational
10.10.1940	3./Kü.Fl.Gr. 606	Do 17 Z-3	3618		7T+KL	Operational
10.10.1940	1./KG 2	Do 17 Z	3442		U5+CH	Operational
10.10.1940	4./KG 2	Do 17 Z-2	1201		U5+BM	Operational
10.10.1940	7./KG 3	Do 17 Z	3293		5K+AR	Operational
11.10.1940	1./Kü.Fl.Gr. 606	Do 17 Z-3	2772		7T+EH	Operational
11.10.1940	1./Kü.Fl.Gr. 606	Do 17 Z-5	2787		7T+HH	Operational
11.10.1940	2./Kü.Fl.Gr. 606	Do 17 Z-3	3475		7T+EK	Operational
11.10.1940	5./KG 2	Do 17 Z	2893		U5+AN	Non-operational
14.10.1940	9./KG 2	Do 17 Z	2556		U5+BT	Operational

DORNIER Do 17 AIRCRAFT CASUALTIES

Country	Location	Details
France	Bouly	Force-landed. Damage 70%.
Holland	Zuidlangeweg, S Colijnsplaat, 10 km NE Noord-Beveland	Attacked by friendly fighter. Damage 80%.
France	Airfield – Cormeilles-en-Vexin	Landing accident in bad weather. Damage 50%.
France	Near Hénonville, 18 km NNW Pontoise	Crashed. Total loss.
France	Haudivillers, 13 km NE Beauvais	Hit ground during night training flight. Total loss.
France	Saint-Pol	Crashed due to lack of fuel and bad weather. Total loss.
France	Airfield – Dinard	Landing accident. Damage 40%.
Belgium	Near Hamme-Mille, 10 km NE Wavre	Crashed. Total loss.
United Kingdom	Snape Wood, Wadhurst, East Sussex	Probably shot down by 253 Squadron. Total loss.
France	2 km E Airfield – Le Bourget	Caught fire on take off and crashed. Total loss.
France	Airfield – Saint-Michel	Landing accident. Damage 40%.
United Kingdom	North Sea, 1 km north of Rattray Head, S Frazerburgh, Aberdeenshire	Ditched after engine failure. Total loss.
France	Grève	Unknown. Total loss.
France	Airfield – Brest	Landing accident. Damage 15%.
United Kingdom	Brighton	Combat with 92 Squadron. Damage 10%.
France	Airfield – Saint-Léger	Landing accident following engine failure. Damage 70%.
Holland	Nijmegen	Crashed after getting lost and fuel shortage. Total loss.
United Kingdom	25 km NW Bardsey Island, North Wales	Shot down by 611 Squadron. Total loss.
France	Airfield – Brest	Damaged in combat with 611 Squadron. Damage 45%.
United Kingdom	Near Liverpool	Shot down by 611 Squadron. Total loss.
France	L'Aisne, 7 km ENE Compiègne	Crashed on navigational flight. Total loss.
France	Airfield – Cambrai-Süd	Landing accident. Damage 25%.

DORNIER Do 17 IN THE BATTLE OF BRITAIN

Date	Unit	Type	W/NR	SKZ	Codes	Duty
14.10.1940	2./KG 3	Do 17 Z-2	1173		5K+FK	Operational
14.10.1940	2./NJG 2	Do 17 Z-10	2851		R4+DK	Operational
16.10.1940	2./Kü.Fl.Gr. 606	Do 17 Z-3	2691		7T+HK	Operational
16.10.1940	3./Kü.Fl.Gr. 606	Do 17 Z-3	2682		7T+LL	Operational
16.10.1940	6./KG 2	Do 17 Z-3	3352		U5+CC	Operational
16.10.1940	6./KG 3	Do 17 Z-3	4252		5K+.P	Operational
16.10.1940	1./KG 76	Do 17 Z-3	3448		F1+FH	Operational
17.10.1940	Stabsst./KG 2	Do 17 Z-2	3349		U5+EA	Operational
18.10.1940	8./KG 2	Do 17 Z-3	2876			Operational
18.10.1940	Stabsst./KG 2	Do 17 Z-3	2674			Operational
19.10.1940	Kü.Fl.Gr. 606	Do 17 Z-2	1210			Operational
19.10.1940	8./KG 2	Do 17 Z-2	1153			Non-operational
19.10.1940	8./KG 2	Do 17 Z-2	3432			Operational
21.10.1940	7./KG 76	Do 17 Z	3397		F1+LS	Operational
22.10.1940	1./Kü.Fl.Gr. 606	Do 17 Z-5	2783		7T+AH	Operational
23.10.1940	9./KG 3	Do 17 Z-2	3362			Operational
24.10.1940	1./KG 2	Do 17 Z	2598			Operational
24.10.1940	1./KG 2	Do 17 Z	3444			Operational
24.10.1940	9./KG 2	Do 17 Z-2	2863			Operational
25.10.1940	3.(F)/11	Do 17 P-1	4073		6M+JL	Operational
25.10.1940	4.(F)/14	Do 17 P	4158		5F+KM	Operational
25.10.1940	8./KG 76	Do 17 Z	2882			Operational
27.10.1940	3./KG 2	Do 17 Z-2	3443		U5+HL	Operational
27.10.1940	7./KG 3	Do 17 Z				Operational
27.10.1940	9./KG 3	Do 17 Z				Operational

DORNIER Do 17 AIRCRAFT CASUALTIES

Country	Location	Details
Belgium	Airfield – Le Culot	Engine failuire on take off. Damage 45%.
Holland	Airfield – Gilze-Rijen	Pilot error in ground fog. Damage 80%.
United Kingdom	Maesbury Ring, Croscomber, Somerset	Crashed following fuel shortage Total loss.
United Kingdom	Hafodwen Farm, Nantglyn, Denbighshire	Hit ground in fog. Total loss.
France	Saint-Léger	Possibly damaged by 249 Squadron. Damage 40%.
Belgium	Antwerp	Hit ground. Damage 30%.
France	Oroër, 4 km N Nivilliers, 6 km NE Beauvais	Crashed at night in bad weather following pilot error and burned out. Total loss.
France	3 km nördlich Ns, 3 km SW Saint-Léger	Crashed. Total loss.
France	Saint-Romain	Force-landed. Damage 40%.
Germany	Kalkar, near Kleve	Hit obstacle and force-landed. Total loss.
France	Airfield – Brest-Süd	Landing accident. Damage 30%.
France	Cambrai	Crashed due to pilot error. Damage 75%.
France	Cambrai	Crashed on landing after combat with 213 Squadron. Damage 40%.
United Kingdom	London	Unknown. Total loss.
United Kingdom	Ness Point, Erwarton, Suffolk	Landed after crew became lost and ran out of fuel. Total loss.
Belgium	Esneux, 12 km S Liège	Crashed following fuel shortage Total loss.
France	L'écluse, 11 km SSW Douai	Crashed in ground fog and burned out. Damage 90%.
France	Sancourt, 5 km NW Cambrai	Pilot error and burned out. Damage 90%.
France	Cambrai	Landing accident after combat with 229 Squadron. Damage 80%.
France	Zutkerque	Burst tyre and ended up on its nose. Damage 30%.
France	3 km SW airfield – Plumetot	Crashed after take off. Total loss.
France	Airfield – Cormeilles-en-Vexin	Crashed and burned out. Total loss.
United Kingdom	Near Bury St. Edmunds	Combat. Damage 5%.
United Kingdom	Airfield – Feltwell	Flak. Damage ?%.
United Kingdom	Airfield – Feltwell	Flak. Damage ?%.

DORNIER Do 17 IN THE BATTLE OF BRITAIN

Date	Unit	Type	W/NR	SKZ	Codes	Duty
27.10.1940	7./KG 76	Do 17 Z-2	1150		F1+HR	Operational
28.10.1940	Kü.Fl.Gr. 606	Do 17 Z	3437			Operational
28.10.1940	1./KG 3	Do 17 Z-2	2544		5K+CH	Operational
28.10.1940	8./KG 3	Do 17 Z				Operational
29.10.1940	3.(F)/31	Do 17 P	3553		5D+HL	Non-operational
29.10.1940	2./KG 3	Do 17 Z-2	3406			Operational
30.10.1940	3.(F)/10	Do 17 P				Operational
30.10.1940	2./KG 3	Do 17 Z-3	2617			Operational
31.10.1940	III/KG 76	Do 17 Z	2367			Operational
31.10.1940	III/KG 76	Do 17 Z	2886			Operational

DORNIER Do 17 AIRCRAFT CASUALTIES

Country	Location	Details
United Kingdom	Holbrook Creek, River Stour, Essex	Shot down by 17 Squadron and Flak. Total loss.
France	Airfield – Brest	Landing accident. Damage 40%.
United Kingdom	Boughton Malherbe, 15 km NW Ashford, Kent	Force-landed following Flak damage. Total loss.
United Kingdom	Channel	Combat. Damage ?%.
France	Orleans	Dusk landing accident. Damage 50%.
Belgium	Le Culot	Landing accident following technical problems. Damage 35%.
United Kingdom	Dover	Flak. Damage 5%.
Belgium	Herentals, 31 km ESE Antwerp	Crashed following fuel shortage Total loss.
France	Compiègne	Crashed following fuel shortage Total loss.
France	Sedan	Crashed following fuel shortage Total loss.

Chapter 5

Dornier Do 17 Crew Casualties

Date	Unit	Type	W/Nr	Codes	Name	Role
3.7.1940	Stab KG 2	Do 17 Z		U5+EA	Reiß, Hans	Beobachter
3.7.1940	Stab KG 2	Do 17 Z		U5+EA	Wagner, Günter	Flugzeugführer
3.7.1940	3./KG 3	Do 17 Z			Chrapkowski, Wolfgang	Flugzeugführer
3.7.1940	3./KG 3	Do 17 Z			Heberle, Georg	Bordmechaniker
3.7.1940	3./KG 3	Do 17 Z			Kretzschmar, Otto	Hilfsbeobachter
3.7.1940	3./KG 3	Do 17 Z			Pohl, Rudolf	Bordfunker
3.7.1940	1./KG 77	Do 17 Z			Birke, Kurt	Hilfsbeobachter
3.7.1940	1./KG 77	Do 17 Z			Dietel, Kurt	Bordschütze
3.7.1940	1./KG 77	Do 17 Z			Flügel, Johannes	Bordfunker
3.7.1940	1./KG 77	Do 17 Z			Steiner, Kurt	Flugzeugführer
3.7.1940	2./KG 77	Do 17 Z			Joppich, Gerhard	Bordfunker
3.7.1940	2./KG 77	Do 17 Z			Kretschmar, Fritz	Beobachter
3.7.1940	2./KG 77	Do 17 Z			Penzel, Alfred	Bordmechaniker
3.7.1940	2./KG 77	Do 17 Z			Saft, Richard	Flugzeugführer
3.7.1940	7./KG 77	Do 17 Z			Gerber, Oskar	
3.7.1940	8./KG 77	Do 17 Z	2642	3Z+GS	Brandes, Richard	Flugzeugführer
3.7.1940	8./KG 77	Do 17 Z	2642	3Z+GS	Gallion, Hans-Georg	Beobachter
3.7.1940	8./KG 77	Do 17 Z	2642	3Z+GS	Hofmann, Erich	Bordfunker
3.7.1940	8./KG 77	Do 17 Z	2642	3Z+GS	Theilig, Waldemar	Bordschütze
3.7.1940	8./KG 77	Do 17 Z			Kuske, Wilhelm	Hilfsbeobachter
3.7.1940	8./KG 77	Do 17 Z			Mair, Walter	Bordschütze

xec	Rank	Fate	Burial	Notes
	Lt	Wounded		
	Ofw	Wounded		
	Oblt	+		
	Fw	+		Body washed ashore
	Fw	Missing		
	Fw	+	Borkum, Grave 632	Body washed ashore 20.08.1940
	Ofw	Missing		
	Gefr	Missing		
	Uffz	+		
	Oblt	Missing		
	Fw	+	Bourdon/France, Block 17, Row 11, Grave 390	
	Oblt	Missing		
	Ofw	Missing		
	Fw	+		
	Uffz	Wounded		
	Uffz	PoW		
	Oblt	PoW		
	Obgfr	+	Cannock Chase/UK, Block 1, Row 7, Grave 248	
	Uffz	+	Cannock Chase/UK, Block 1, Row 7, Grave 249	
	Uffz	+	Bourdon/France, Block 25, Row 16, Grave 619	
	Gefr	+	Bourdon/France, Block 25, Row 15, Grave 572	

DORNIER Do 17 IN THE BATTLE OF BRITAIN

Date	Unit	Type	W/Nr	Codes	Name	Role
3.7.1940	8./KG 77	Do 17 Z			Patrzich, Werner	Flugzeugführer
3.7.1940	8./KG 77	Do 17 Z			Pfeiffer, Rudolf	Bordfunker
3.7.1940	9./KG 77	Do 17 Z			Goldhorn, Ernst	Bordmechanike
3.7.1940	9./KG 77	Do 17 Z			Kapsch, Hermann	Flugzeugführer
3.7.1940	9./KG 77	Do 17 Z			Schwarzbach, Karl	Hilfsbeobachte
3.7.1940	9./KG 77	Do 17 Z			Thiemicke, Kurt	Bordfunker
4.7.1940	6./KG 2	Do 17 Z			Behrer, Alois	Bordfunker
4.7.1940	6./KG 2	Do 17 Z			Reitter, Helmut	Bordschütze
4.7.1940	6./KG 2	Do 17 Z			Riediger, Wolf-Dietrich	Beobachter
4.7.1940	Stab II/KG 2	Do 17 Z			Dörwaldt, Friedrich	Beobachter
4.7.1940	Stab II/KG 2	Do 17 Z			Krehl, Helmut	Bordfunker
4.7.1940	Stab II/KG 2	Do 17 Z			Wolff, Hans	Flugzeugführer
4.7.1940	4./KG 77	Do 17 Z			Boost, Heinz	Bordfunker
4.7.1940	4./KG 77	Do 17 Z			Eichhorn, Ludwig	Flugzeugführer
4.7.1940	4./KG 77	Do 17 Z			Hartmann, Gerhard	Hilfsbeobachte
4.7.1940	4./KG 77	Do 17 Z			Hollerauer, Georg	Bordmechanike
6.7.1940	1.(F)/120	Do 17 P		A6+JH	Enke, Werner	
6.7.1940	1.(F)/120	Do 17 P		A6+JH	Gapp, Leopold	
7.7.1940	2.(F)/11	Do 17 P-1		6M+AK	Dehner, Helmut	Beobachter
7.7.1940	2.(F)/11	Do 17 P-1		6M+AK	Moritz, Gerhard	Flugzeugführer
7.7.1940	2.(F)/11	Do 17 P-1		6M+AK	Pfeil, Max	Bordfunker
7.7.1940	4.(F)/121	Do 17 P		7A+FM	Wingert, Paul	Bordfunker
7.7.1940	2.(F)/123	Do 17 P		4U+KK	Plotzitzka, Walter	Flugzeugführer
7.7.1940	2.(F)/123	Do 17 P		4U+KK	Scherzinger, Rudolf	Beobachter
7.7.1940	2.(F)/123	Do 17 P		4U+KK	Storch, Richard	Bordfunker
7.7.1940	2.(F)/123	Do 17 P		4U+FK	Elicker, Friedrich-Wilhelm	Bordfunker

140

DORNIER Do 17 CREW CASUALTIES

xec	Rank	Fate	Burial	Notes
	Fw	+	Bourdon/France, Block 25, Row 15, Grave 571	
	Uffz	+	Bourdon/France, Block 19, Row 4, Grave 133	
	Uffz	Wounded		
	Oblt	Wounded		
	Uffz	Wounded		
	Gefr	Wounded		
	Fw	Wounded		
	Gefr			
	Lt	Wounded		
	Oblt	Wounded		
	Uffz	Wounded		
	Ofw			
	Uffz	+		
	Fw	+	Bourdon/France, Block 30, Row 13, Grave 515	
	Uffz	+	Bourdon/France, Block 30, Row 13, Grave 513	
	Uffz	+	Bourdon/France, Block 30, Row 13, Grave 531	
	Uffz	Interned		
	Uffz	Interned		
	Ofw	+		
	Fw	+		
	Fw	+		
	Ogfr	Wounded		
	Fw	+		Body washed ashore 04.08.1940
	Fw	Missing		
		Missing		
	Uffz	Missing		

DORNIER Do 17 IN THE BATTLE OF BRITAIN

Date	Unit	Type	W/Nr	Codes	Name	Role
7.7.1940	2.(F)/123	Do 17 P		4U+FK	Nest, Hans-Joachim	Flugzeugführer
7.7.1940	2.(F)/123	Do 17 P		4U+FK	Vedder, Bernhard	Beobachter
7.7.1940	4./KG 2	Do 17 Z			Seidel, Johannes	Beobachter
8.7.1940	5./KG 3	Do 17 Z			Honerlagen, Wilhelm	Feinmech.
8.7.1940	5./KG 3	Do 17 Z			Kästner, Erich	Flzg.-Mech.
8.7.1940	5./KG 3	Do 17 Z			Unferfert, Gerhard	Bordfunker
9.7.1940	4./KG 3	Do 17 Z-2			Kostropetsch, Fritz	Bombenschütze
9.7.1940	4./KG 3	Do 17 Z-2			Schneider, Johannes	Bordschütze
9.7.1940	Stabsst./ KG 76	Do 17 Z		F1+BA	Lemke, Hans	Bordfunker
9.7.1940	Stabsst./ KG 76	Do 17 Z		F1+BA	Sankowski, Werner	Bordmechanike
9.7.1940	1./NJG 1	Do 17		2N+CH	Hagmeier, Heinrich	Bordfunker
9.7.1940	1./NJG 1	Do 17		2N+CH	Iburg, Adolf	Flugzeugführer
10.7.1940	4.(F)/121	Do 17 P-1			Fränzis, Willi	Bordfunker
10.7.1940	4.(F)/121	Do 17 P-1			Somborn, Otto	Beobachter
10.7.1940	1./KG 2	Do 17 Z			Assum, Martin	Bordfunker
10.7.1940	1./KG 2	Do 17 Z			Deckarm, Karl	Beobachter
10.7.1940	1./KG 2	Do 17 Z			Enderle, Franz	Bordmechanike
10.7.1940	1./KG 2	Do 17 Z			Kröhl, Georg	Flugzeugführer
10.7.1940	2./KG 2	Do 17 Z			Schmidt, Rudolf	Beobachter
10.7.1940	2./KG 2	Do 17 Z			Althaus, Gerhard	Bordfunker
10.7.1940	2./KG 2	Do 17 Z			Schmitz, Rudolf	Bordmechanike
10.7.1940	3./KG 2	Do 17 Z		U5+HL	Broich, Peter	Flugzeugführer
10.7.1940	3./KG 2	Do 17 Z		U5+HL	Meyer, Karl	Bordfunker
10.7.1940	3./KG 2	Do 17 Z		U5+HL	Seßner, Wilhelm	Beobachter
10.7.1940	3./KG 2	Do 17 Z		U5+HL	Süptitz, Walter	Bordmechanike
10.7.1940	3./KG 2	Do 17 Z		U5+FL	Krieger, Walter	Beobachter
10.7.1940	3./KG 2	Do 17 Z		U5+FL	Osinsky, Horst	Bordmechanike
10.7.1940	3./KG 2	Do 17 Z		U5+FL	Thalmann, Werner	Bordfunker

DORNIER Do 17 CREW CASUALTIES

Exec	Rank	Fate	Burial	Notes
	Lt	Missing		
	Lt	+	Lommel/Belgium, Block 61, Grave 548	
	Oblt	Wounded		
	Flg	Wounded		
	Ogfr	Wounded		
	Ofw	Wounded		
	Uffz	Wounded		
	Gefr	Wounded/+		
	Fw	Wounded		
	Fw	Wounded		
	Uffz			
	Fw			
	Gefr	Wounded		
	Oblt	+		
	Gefr	Wounded		
	Ofw			
	Fw	+	Lommel/Belgium, Block 43, Grave 301	
	Obgfr	Wounded		
	Fw	+	Bourdon/France, Block 8, Row 9, Grave 317	
	Uffz	Wounded		
	Uffz	Wounded		
	Fw	Wounded		
	Uffz	Wounded		
	Uffz			
	Uffz	+	Lommel/Belgium, Block 43, Grave 291	
Kap	Hptm	PoW		
	Fw	Missing		
	Ofw	PoW		

DORNIER Do 17 IN THE BATTLE OF BRITAIN

Date	Unit	Type	W/Nr	Codes	Name	Role
10.7.1940	3./KG 2	Do 17 Z		U5+FL	Winkelmann, Karl	Flugzeugführer
10.7.1940	4./KG 3	Do 17 Z			Bott, Hilmar	Flugzeugführer
10.7.1940	4./KG 3	Do 17 Z			Frenz, Edi	Bordmechanike
10.7.1940	4./KG 3	Do 17 Z			Puk, Franz	Bordfunker
10.7.1940	4./KG 3	Do 17 Z			Schröder, Friedrich-Karl	Beobachter
11.7.1940	2.(F)/11	Do 17 P-1			Möckel, Erich	Flugzeugführer
11.7.1940	2.(F)/11	Do 17 P-1			Oberschmidt, Karl	Bordfunker
11.7.1940	2.(F)/11	Do 17 P-1			Wähner, Max	Beobachter
11.7.1940	4./KG 2	Do 17 Z		U5+GM	Borner, Werner	Bordfunker
11.7.1940	4./KG 2	Do 17 Z		U5+GM	Bornschein, Walter	Beobachter
11.7.1940	4./KG 2	Do 17 Z		U5+GM	Genzow, Joachim	Flugzeugführer
11.7.1940	4./KG 2	Do 17 Z		U5+GM	Lohrer, Friedrich	Bordmechanike
11.7.1940	1./KG 3	Do 17 Z			Fischer, Hans	Beobachter
11.7.1940	Wekusta 26	Do 17			Bauer, Arthur	Bordfunker
11.7.1940	Wekusta 26	Do 17			Belger, Wilhelm	Meteorologe
11.7.1940	Wekusta 26	Do 17			Deike, Reinhold	Bordmechanike
11.7.1940	Wekusta 26	Do 17			Haase, Karl	Flugzeugführer
12.7.1940	5./KG 2	Do 17 Z			Eidenberger, Wilhelm	Bordfunker
12.7.1940	5./KG 2	Do 17 Z			Lepszy, Siegfried	Beobachter
12.7.1940	5./KG 2	Do 17 Z			Loges, Fritz	Bordmechanike
12.7.1940	5./KG 2	Do 17 Z			Zelmer, Arno	Flugzeugführer
12.7.1940	5./KG 2	Do 17 Z			Latzke, Erich	Bordfunker
12.7.1940	5./KG 2	Do 17 Z			Machetzki, Erich	Flugzeugführer
12.7.1940	5./KG 2	Do 17 Z			Rohr, Hermann	Bordmechanike
12.7.1940	5./KG 2	Do 17 Z			Röwe, Heinz	Beobachter
13.7.1940	2.(F)/123	Do 17 P		4U+DK	Graf von Kesselstatt, M	Beobachter
13.7.1940	2.(F)/123	Do 17 P		4U+DK	Peelen, Gerhard	Bordfunker
13.7.1940	2.(F)/123	Do 17 P		4U+DK	Weinbauer, Oskar	Flugzeugführer

xec	Rank	Fate	Burial	Notes
	Fw	Missing		
	Oblt	+		
	Gefr	+		Body washed ashore 03.08.1940
	Ofw	Missing		
	Lt	+	Ysselsteyn/Holland, Block AQ, Row 12, Grave 282	
	Fw	Missing		
	Gefr	Missing		
	Uffz	Missing		
	Fw	Wounded		
	Lt	Wounded		
	Oblt			
	Fw	Wounded		
	Lt	Wounded		
	Gefr	Missing		
	Reg.Rat	Missing		
	Uffz	Missing		
	Uffz	Missing		
	Uffz	Missing		
	Ofw	Missing		
	Uffz	Wounded		
	Fw	Missing		
	Uffz	Missing		
Kap	Hptm	Missing		
	Uffz	Missing		
	Oblt	Missing		
	Oblt	PoW		
	Fw	+	Cannock Chase/UK, Block 6, Row 18, Grave 366	
	Lt	+	Cannock Chase/UK, Block 6, Row 18, Grave 367	

Date	Unit	Type	W/Nr	Codes	Name	Role
18.7.1940	Stabsst./ St.G 77	Do 17 M			Greil, Alois	Flugzeugführer
18.7.1940	Stabsst./ St.G 77	Do 17 M			Strecker, Heinz	Beobachter
18.7.1940	Stabsst./ St.G 77	Do 17 M			Strehle, Max	Bordfunker
19.7.1940	4.(F)/121	Do 17 P	1098	7A+CM	Manko, Erich	Bordfunker
19.7.1940	4.(F)/121	Do 17 P	1098	7A+CM	Roos, Rupprecht	Flugzeugführer
19.7.1940	4.(F)/121	Do 17 P	1098	7A+CM	Thiele, Walter	Beobachter
20.7.1940	1.(F)/120	Do 17 P-1		A6+HH	Bergmann, Gerhard	Bordfunker
20.7.1940	1.(F)/120	Do 17 P-1		A6+HH	Heuer, Hubert	Flugzeugführer
20.7.1940	1.(F)/120	Do 17 P-1		A6+HH	Hinz, Walter	Beobachter
20.7.1940	9./KG 2	Do 17 Z			Davids, Bruno	Beobachter
20.7.1940	9./KG 2	Do 17 Z			Mewe, Ernst	Bordmechanike
20.7.1940	Stabsst./ St.G 2	Do 17 M			Fengels, Herrmann	Flugzeugführer
20.7.1940	Stabsst./ St.G 2	Do 17 M			Schenkel, Herbert	Beobachter
20.7.1940	Stabsst./ St.G 2	Do 17 M			Schleifer, Ottmar	Bordfunker
21.7.1940	4.(F)/14	Do 17 M		5F+OM	Bohnen, Fritz	Flugzeugführer
21.7.1940	4.(F)/14	Do 17 M		5F+OM	Thiel, Georg	Beobachter
21.7.1940	4.(F)/14	Do 17 M		5F+OM	Werner, Alfred	Bordfunker
21.7.1940	9./KG 3	Do 17 Z		5K+ET	Erharter, Kaspar	Bombenschütze
21.7.1940	9./KG 3	Do 17 Z		5K+ET	Lauffer, Hans	Flugzeugführer
21.7.1940	9./KG 3	Do 17 Z		5K+ET	Paulisch, Horst	Bordschütze
22.7.1940	4.(F)/121	Do 17 P	3598	7A+DM	Bormann, Gert	Flugzeugführer
22.7.1940	4.(F)/121	Do 17 P	3598	7A+DM	Reichardt, Erwin	Beobachter
22.7.1940	4.(F)/121	Do 17 P	3598	7A+DM	Rowe, Reinhard	Bordfunker
23.7.1940	1./Kü.Fl.Gr. 606	Do 17 Z-3	3487	7T+BH	Germann, Helmut	Flugzeugführer
23.7.1940	1./Kü.Fl.Gr. 606	Do 17 Z-3	3487	7T+BH	Hermann-Geschke, Otto	Beobachter

DORNIER Do 17 CREW CASUALTIES

xec	Rank	Fate	Burial	Notes
	Fw	Missing		
	Oblt	+	Champigny-St.Andre/France, Block 10, Grave 1158	Body washed ashore 18.07.1940
	Uffz	+		
	Obgfr	+		
	Uffz	Missing		
	Lt	Missing		
	Uffz	Missing		
	Lt	+		
	Fw	Missing		
Kap	Oblt	Wounded		
	Ofw	+	Bourdon/France, Block 22, Row 3, Grave 97	
	Fw	Wounded		
	Lt	Wounded		
	Fw	+		
	Fw	PoW		
	Oblt	PoW		
	Uffz	PoW		
	Uffz	+		
	Uffz	+		
	Gefr	+		
	Lt	PoW		
	Lt	+		
	Fw	+		
	Uffz	Missing		
	Lt.z.S	Missing		

DORNIER Do 17 IN THE BATTLE OF BRITAIN

Date	Unit	Type	W/Nr	Codes	Name	Role
23.7.1940	1./Kü.Fl.Gr. 606	Do 17 Z-3	3487	7T+BH	Olson, Werner	Bordmechaniker
23.7.1940	1./Kü.Fl.Gr. 606	Do 17 Z-3	3487	7T+BH	Trampler, Erich	Bordfunker
23.7.1940	2./KG 3	Do 17 Z			Kahlfuß, Bruno	Flugzeugführer
23.7.1940	2./KG 3	Do 17 Z			Kellmann, Josef	Bordfunker
23.7.1940	2./KG 3	Do 17 Z			Reinhardt, Herbert	Bordschütze
23.7.1940	2./KG 3	Do 17 Z			Strecker	Beobachter
24.7.1940	5./KG 2	Do 17 Z			Mischke, Johannes	Bordfunker
24.7.1940	5./KG 2	Do 17 Z			Zarbeck, Otto	Flugzeugführer
25.7.1940	Stabsst./ St.G 1	Do 17 M		A5+EA	Erdmann, Bernhard	Flugzeugführer
25.7.1940	Stabsst./ St.G 1	Do 17 M		A5+EA	Großmann, Erich	Beobachter
25.7.1940	Stabsst./ St.G 1	Do 17 M		A5+EA	Lingenbrink, Kurt	Bordfunker
26.7.1940	4./KG 3	Do 17 Z-3			Schrader, Paul-Georg	Beobachter
26.7.1940	3./KG 76	Do 17 Z			Ballowitz, Bernhard	Bordfunker
26.7.1940	3./KG 76	Do 17 Z			Bungardt, Heinrich	Bombenschütze
26.7.1940	3./KG 76	Do 17 Z			Hartz, Friedrich	Flugzeugführer
26.7.1940	3./KG 76	Do 17 Z			Kopisch, Heinrich	Bordmechaniker
27.7.1940	2./NJG 2	Do 17 Z-7	2834	2N+GH	Buck, Gustav	Flugzeugführer
27.7.1940	2./NJG 2	Do 17 Z-7	2834	2N+GH	Schmidt, Hermann	Bordfunker
29.7.1940	6./KG 2	Do 17 Z			Mazunat, Paul	Flugzeugführer
29.7.1940	Stabsst./ KG 2	Do 17 Z			Hunger, Heinrich	Flugzeugführer
29.7.1940	Stab III/KG 76	Do 17 Z			Genth, Adolf	Beobachter
29.7.1940	Stab III/KG 76	Do 17 Z			Riebl, Edmund	Flugzeugführer
30.7.1940	2./KG 76	Do 17 Z		F1+AK	Dießner, Adolf	Bordfunker

DORNIER Do 17 CREW CASUALTIES

xec	Rank	Fate	Burial	Notes
	Uffz	Missing		
	Ofw	Missing		
	Uffz	Wounded		From Stabsst./ KG 3
	Ogfr	Wounded		From Stabsst./ KG 3
	Fw			
	Uffz	Wounded		
	Uffz	Wounded		
	Fw	PoW		
	Fw	PoW		
	Uffz	+	Cannock Chase/England, Block 6, Row 18, Grave 368	
	Oblt	Wounded		
	Ofw	Missing		
	Uffz	Missing		
	Uffz	Missing		
	Fw	Missing		
	Fw	+		
	Fw	+	Lüdenscheid-Am Wehberg-Ev.Cemetery, Block C, Row 2, Grave 3	
	Obgfr	+		
	Lt			
r Kdr	Oberstlt	Wounded/+		
	Ofw			
	Fw	+	Beauvais/France, Block 1, Row 3, Grave 96	

Date	Unit	Type	W/Nr	Codes	Name	Role
30.7.1940	2./KG 76	Do 17 Z		F1+AK	Pungor, Josef	Bordschütze
30.7.1940	2./KG 76	Do 17 Z		F1+AK	Schmid, Hans	Flugzeugführer
30.7.1940	2./KG 76	Do 17 Z		F1+AK	von Kaler, Rudolf	Bombenschütze
2.8.1940	Stabsst./ St.G 3	Do 17 M		V4+FA	Kusko	Beobachter
3.8.1940	4.(F)/14	Do 17 P			Poppe, Adolf	Bordfunker
3.8.1940	4.(F)/14	Do 17 P			Schaefer, Hellmuth	Beobachter
3.8.1940	4.(F)/14	Do 17 P			Völkel, Rolf	Flugzeugführer
3.8.1940	Stabsst./ St.G 3	Do 17 M			Krause, Willy	Flugzeugführer
3.8.1940	Stabsst./ St.G 3	Do 17 M			Küster, Helmut	Beobachter
3.8.1940	Stabsst./ St.G 3	Do 17 M			Sellke, Ernst	Bordfunker
5.8.1940	9./KG 3	Do 17 Z-2	3350	5K+AT	Pierschel, Heinrich	Waffenwart
5.8.1940	9./KG 3	Do 17 Z-2	3350	5K+AT	Potrawa, Hans	Hilfsbeobachter
5.8.1940	9./KG 3	Do 17 Z-2	3350	5K+AT	Schneider, Heinrich	Flugzeugführer
5.8.1940	9./KG 3	Do 17 Z-2	3350	5K+AT	Weiß, Gerhard	Bordfunker
6.8.1940	7./KG 3	Do 17 Z		5K+AR	Berg, Willi	Bordschütze
6.8.1940	7./KG 3	Do 17 Z		5K+AR	Ullrich, Karl	Flugzeugführer
6.8.1940	7./KG 3	Do 17 Z		5K+AR	Weiß, Fritz	Bordfunker
6.8.1940	7./KG 3	Do 17 Z		5K+AR	Widera, Kurt	Hilfsbeobachter
9.8.1940	3.(F)/11	Do 17 P-1		6M+GL	Hoh, Hellmut	Flugzeugführer
9.8.1940	3.(F)/11	Do 17 P-1		6M+GL	Thiel, Hans-Joachim	Beobachter
9.8.1940	3.(F)/11	Do 17 P-1		6M+GL	Wergin, Josef	Bordfunker
11.8.1940	9./KG 2	Do 17 Z			Lipinski, Gerhard	Bordfunker
11.8.1940	9./KG 2	Do 17 Z			Lenz, Richard	Bordmechaniker
11.8.1940	9./KG 2	Do 17 Z			Uhl, Josef	Hilfsbeobachter
11.8.1940	9./KG 2	Do 17 Z			Schmidt, Herbert	Hilfsbeobachter

DORNIER Do 17 CREW CASUALTIES

xec	Rank	Fate	Burial	Notes
	Uffz	+	Beauvais/France, Block 1, Row 3, Grave 98	
	Uffz	+		
	Ogfr	+	Beauvais/France, Block 1, Row 3, Grave 99	
	Oblt	+		
	Fw	Missing		
	Oblt	+	Champigny-St.Andre/France, Block 6, Row 12, Grave 971	
	Oblt	+		
	Fw	+		
	Olt	+		
	Uffz	+		
	Uffz	+	Dresden-Nordfriedhof, Block E, Row 6, Grave 12	
	Fw	+		
	Uffz	+		
	Uffz	+	Hamburg-Ohlsdorf, Block Z34, Grave 23	
	Gefr	Missing		
	Oblt	Missing		
	Uffz	Missing		
	Fw	Missing		
	Lt	Wounded		
	Lt	Wounded		
	Uffz	Wounded		
	Uffz	+	Bourdon/France, Block 22, Row 6, Grave 203	
	Uffz	Wounded		
	Gefr	Wounded		
	Fw	Wounded		

DORNIER Do 17 IN THE BATTLE OF BRITAIN

Date	Unit	Type	W/Nr	Codes	Name	Role
11.8.1940	9./KG 4	Do 17 Z			Reimers, Wilhelm	Bordfunker
12.8.1940	3./KG 2	Do 17 Z			Hoffmann, Kurt	Hilfsbeobachter
12.8.1940	3./KG 2	Do 17 Z			Kaube, Helmut	Bordfunker
12.8.1940	3./KG 2	Do 17 Z			Knop, Hermann	Flugzeugführer
12.8.1940	3./KG 2	Do 17 Z			Woitzik, Hans	Bordmechaniker
12.8.1940	4./KG 2	Do 17 Z			Bürkner	Flugzeugführer
12.8.1940	4./KG 2	Do 17 Z			Reitter, Helmut	Bordschütze
12.8.1940	4./KG 2	Do 17 Z			Schlegel, Willi	Bordfunker
12.8.1940	4./KG 2	Do 17 Z			Dehmel, Kurt	Bordmechaniker
12.8.1940	9./KG 2	Do 17 Z			Heutz, Josef	Bordmechanik
13.8.1940	3.(F)/22	Do 17 P			Bauer, Hans	Bordfunker
13.8.1940	3.(F)/22	Do 17 P			Otto, Helmut	Beobachter
13.8.1940	3.(F)/22	Do 17 P			Panhans, Reinhold	Flugzeugführer
13.8.1940	7./KG 2	Do 17 Z		U5+FR	Beck, Alfred	Bordmechanik
13.8.1940	7./KG 2	Do 17 Z		U5+FR	Dannich, Franz	Flugzeugführer
13.8.1940	7./KG 2	Do 17 Z		U5+FR	Nitzsche, Erich	Bordfunker
13.8.1940	7./KG 2	Do 17 Z		U5+FR	Schwertfeger, Kai	Beobachter
13.8.1940	7./KG 2	Do 17 Z		U5+ER	Arndt, Herbert	Hilfsbeobachter
13.8.1940	7./KG 2	Do 17 Z		U5+ER	Bahr, Helmut	Bordmechanik
13.8.1940	7./KG 2	Do 17 Z		U5+ER	Mähringer, Willy	Bordfunker
13.8.1940	7./KG 2	Do 17 Z		U5+ER	Vogel, Georg	Flugzeugführer
13.8.1940	8./KG 2	Do 17 Z		U5+DS	Haensgen, Rudolf	Bordmechanik
13.8.1940	8./KG 2	Do 17 Z		U5+DS	Langer, Karl	Bordfunker
13.8.1940	8./KG 2	Do 17 Z		U5+DS	Morich, Werner	Beobachter
13.8.1940	8./KG 2	Do 17 Z		U5+DS	Müller, Gerhard	Flugzeugführer

DORNIER Do 17 CREW CASUALTIES

xec	Rank	Fate	Burial	Notes
	Uffz	Wounded/+		
	Uffz	Wounded		
	Uffz	Wounded		
	Fw	Wounded		
	Uffz	Wounded		
	Gefr	Wounded		
	Gefr	Wounded		
	Fw	Wounded		
	Uffz	Wounded		
	Uffz	Missing		
	Fw	Missing		
	Lt	+	Göteborg-Kviberg/Sweden, Block 21, Row 3, Grave 257	Body washed ashore at Långeskär 07.10.1940
	Gefr	+	Cannock Chase/UK, Block 1, Row 11, Grave 420	
	Fw	+	Cannock Chase/UK, Block 1, Row 11, Grave 426	
	Obgfr	+	Cannock Chase/UK, Block 1, Row 11, Grave 422	
	Fw	+	Cannock Chase/UK, Block 1, Row 11, Grave 424	
	Uffz	PoW		
	Gefr	PoW		
	Uffz	PoW		
	Uffz	PoW		
	Fw	PoW		
	Ofw	+	Cannock Chase/England, Block 1, Row 5, Grave 178	Baled out but believed to have died 22.08.1940
Kap	Oblt	+	Cannock Chase/England	
	Oblt	+	Whitstable Cemetery/England	

DORNIER Do 17 IN THE BATTLE OF BRITAIN

Date	Unit	Type	W/Nr	Codes	Name	Role
13.8.1940	8./KG 2	Do 17 Z			Bensch, Karl-Heinz	Flugzeugführer
13.8.1940	8./KG 2	Do 17 Z			Radlach, Ekkehard	Hilfsbeobachter
13.8.1940	8./KG 2	Do 17 Z			Gizinski, Erhard	Flugzeugführer
13.8.1940	8./KG 2	Do 17 Z			Sopart, Alfons	Bordfunker
13.8.1940	8./KG 2	Do 17 Z			Schirr, Hermann	Flugzeugführer
13.8.1940	Stab III/ KG 2	Do 17 Z			Böke, Walter	Bordmechaniker
13.8.1940	Stab III/ KG 2	Do 17 Z			Herrmann, Otto	Flugzeugführer
13.8.1940	Stab III/ KG 2	Do 17 Z			Schweinoch, Waldemar	Bordfunker
13.8.1940	Stab III/ KG 2	Do 17 Z			von der Groeben, Horst	Beobachter
13.8.1940	Stabsst. KG 2	Do 17 Z		U5+KA	Babbe, Gustav	Bordfunker
13.8.1940	Stabsst. KG 2	Do 17 Z		U5+KA	Holz, Ernst	Beobachter
13.8.1940	Stabsst. KG 2	Do 17 Z		U5+KA	Oßwald, Gerhard	Beobachter
13.8.1940	Stabsst. KG 2	Do 17 Z		U5+KA	Schlegel, Heinz	Flugzeugführer
13.8.1940	Stabsst. KG 2	Do 17 Z			Däberitz, Kurt	Bordfunker
13.8.1940	Stabsst. KG 2	Do 17 Z			Schilling, Hermann	Bordmechaniker
15.8.1940	3.(F)/31	Do 17 P			Braasch, Karl	
15.8.1940	3.(F)/31	Do 17 P			Gropp, Ernst	
15.8.1940	3.(F)/31	Do 17 P			Horn, Hans	
15.8.1940	2./KG 3	Do 17 Z-2			Schmidt, Erich	Flugzeugführer
15.8.1940	Stab I/KG 3	Do 17 Z-3			Frhr. von Wechmar, Karl	Beobachter
15.8.1940	Stab I/KG 3	Do 17 Z-3			Köhnke, Otto	Flugzeugführer
15.8.1940	6./KG 3	Do 17 Z-2		5K+LP	Depenheuer, Herbert	Bombenschütze
15.8.1940	6./KG 3	Do 17 Z-2		5K+LP	Duda, Wilhelm	

xec	Rank	Fate	Burial	Notes
	Fw	Wounded		
	Fw	Wounded		
	Lt	Wounded		
	Obgfr	Wounded		
	Ofw	Wounded		
	Uffz	+	Bourdon/France, Block 14, Row 1, Grave 18	
	Uffz	+	Lommel/Belgium, Block 63, Grave 32	
	Uffz	+	Bourdon/France, Block 15, Row 12, Grave 434	Body washed ashore
	Oblt	+	Whitstable Cemetery/England	
	Obgfr	PoW		
	Obgfr	PoW		
t Kap	Oblt	PoW		
	Oblt	PoW		
	Gefr	Wounded		
	Fw	Wounded		
	Lt	Missing		
	Gefr	Missing		
	Oblt	Missing		
	Fw	Wounded		
r Kdr	Oberstlt			
	Oblt	Wounded		
	Uffz	+	Cannock Chase/UK, Block 1, Row 11, Grave 419	
	Obgfr	PoW		

DORNIER Do 17 IN THE BATTLE OF BRITAIN

Date	Unit	Type	W/Nr	Codes	Name	Role
15.8.1940	6./KG 3	Do 17 Z-2		5K+LP	Kringler, Heinz	Flugzeugführer
15.8.1940	6./KG 3	Do 17 Z-2		5K+LP	Rohleder, Oskar	
15.8.1940	6./KG 3	Do 17 Z-2			Bruckmann	
15.8.1940	6./KG 3	Do 17 Z-2			Burghardt, Artur	Bombenschütze
15.8.1940	6./KG 3	Do 17 Z-2			Krug, Peter	Flugzeugführer
15.8.1940	6./KG 3	Do 17 Z-2			Reinhardt, Robert	Bordschütze
15.8.1940	6./KG 3	Do 17 Z-2			Kirchübel, Eberhard	Bordfunker
15.8.1940	6./KG 3	Do 17 Z-2			Pieronczyk, Alfons	Bordschütze
15.8.1940	6./KG 3	Do 17 Z-2			Schauer, Fritz	Hlifsbeobachter
15.8.1940	6./KG 3	Do 17 Z-2			Walter, Hans-Eberhard	Flugzeugführer
15.8.1940	6./KG 3	Do 17 Z-2			Fricke, Wilfried	Flugzeugführer
15.8.1940	6./KG 3	Do 17 Z-2			Giehl, Johannes	Bombenschütze
15.8.1940	6./KG 3	Do 17 Z-2			Plesse, Franz	Bordfunker
15.8.1940	Stabsst./KG 76	Do 17 Z			Fröhlich, Stephan	Beobachter
15.8.1940	Stabsst./KG 76	Do 17 Z			Lommatzsch, Hans	Flugzeugführer
15.8.1940	Stabsst./KG 76	Do 17 Z			Winterhalder, Kurt	Hilfsbeobachter
16.8.1940	3./KG 2	Do 17 Z-2		U5+LL	Golob, Johann	Bordschütze
16.8.1940	3./KG 2	Do 17 Z-2		U5+LL	Hess, Philipp	Bombenschütze
16.8.1940	3./KG 2	Do 17 Z-2		U5+LL	Möllenbrock, Heinz-Georg	Flugzeugführer
16.8.1940	3./KG 2	Do 17 Z-2		U5+LL	Reinicke, Gerhard	Bordfunker
16.8.1940	3./KG 2	Do 17 Z-3		U5+BL	Conrad, Carl	Beobachter
16.8.1940	3./KG 2	Do 17 Z-3		U5+BL	Gerlach, Heinz	Flugzeugführer
16.8.1940	3./KG 2	Do 17 Z-3		U5+BL	Holler, Alexander	Bordmechaniker
16.8.1940	3./KG 2	Do 17 Z-3		U5+BL	Krakow, Günther	Bordfunker

DORNIER Do 17 CREW CASUALTIES

xec	Rank	Fate	Burial	Notes
	Lt	+	Cannock Chase/UK, Block 1, Row 11, Grave 418	
	Gefr	PoW	Ramsgate & St. Lawrence Cemetery/UK, Block M, Row A, Grave 77	
	Gefr			
	Gefr			
	Lt			
	Gefr	Wounded		
	Uffz	PoW		
	Uffz	PoW		
	Fw	PoW		
	Lt	PoW		
	Uffz	Wounded		
	Uffz	Wounded		
	Ogfr	Wounded		
eschwaderkommodore	Oberstlt			
	Oblt	Wounded/+		Stab III/ KG 76. Died 07.09.1940
	Fw	Wounded		
	Gefr	+	Cannock Chase/UK, Block 1, Row 2, Grave 38	
	Uffz	PoW		
	Lt	PoW		
	Gefr	+	Cannock Chase/UK, Block 1, Row 2, Grave 37	
	Oblt			
	Ofw			
	Uffz	Wounded		
	Fw	Wounded		

Date	Unit	Type	W/Nr	Codes	Name	Role
16.8.1940	3./KG 2	Do 17 Z-3			Brandenburg, Hans-Jürgen	Flugzeugführer
16.8.1940	3./KG 2	Do 17 Z-3			Genter, Eugen	Beobachter
16.8.1940	3./KG 2	Do 17 Z-3			Hirsch, Kurt	Bordfunker
16.8.1940	3./KG 2	Do 17 Z-3			Koch, Johann	Bordschütze
16.8.1940	Stab III/KG 76	Do 17 Z-2			Brauer, Ernst	Bordmechanike
16.8.1940	Stab III/KG 76	Do 17 Z-2			Klumb, Edmund	Bordfunker
16.8.1940	Stab III/KG 76	Do 17 Z-2			Riebl, Edmund	Flugzeugführer
16.8.1940	Stab III/KG 76	Do 17 Z-2			Wächter, Anton	Beobachter
18.8.1940	6./KG 2	Do 17 Z-3			Linemann, Ulrich	Beobachter
18.8.1940	1./KG 76	Do 17 Z	2504	F1+IH	Beck, Johan	Beobachter
18.8.1940	1./KG 76	Do 17 Z	2504	F1+IH	Gengel, Paul	Bordfunker
18.8.1940	1./KG 76	Do 17 Z	2504	F1+IH	Lautersack, Wilhelm	Bordmechanike
18.8.1940	1./KG 76	Do 17 Z	2504	F1+IH	Stoldt, Walter	Flugzeugführer
18.8.1940	1./KG 76	Do 17 Z	2504	F1+IH	Surk, Walter	Kr.Ber.
18.8.1940	2./KG 76	Do 17 Z			Hanke,	Flugzeugführer
18.8.1940	2./KG 76	Do 17 Z			Dubensky, Wolfgang	Bombenschütze
18.8.1940	3./KG 76	Do 17 Z			Wöhlermann, Eberhard	Flugzeugführer
18.8.1940	3./KG 76	Do 17 Z			Schwarz, Josef	Bordfunker
18.8.1940	8./KG 76	Do 17 Z			Disch, Albert	Bordmechanike
18.8.1940	8./KG 76	Do 17 Z			Leder, Ernst	Flugzeugführer
18.8.1940	8./KG 76	Do 17 Z			Rudolf, Wilhelm	Bordfunker

xec	Rank	Fate	Burial	Notes
	Oblt	+	Cannock Chase/UK, Block 9, Row 8, Grave 49	
	Gefr	+	Cannock Chase/UK, Block 9, Row 8, Grave 49	
	Gefr	+	Cannock Chase/UK, Block 9, Row 8, Grave 49	
	Flg	+	Cannock Chase/UK, Block 9, Row 8, Grave 49	
	Ofw	Missing		
	Fw	+	Tonbridge Cemetery, Kent/ UK, Block S, Grave 15	
	Ofw	Missing		
	Ofw	+	Tonbridge Cemetery, Kent/ UK, Block S, Row F, Grave 15	
	Hptm	Wounded		
	Fw	PoW		
	Uffz	+	Cannock Chase/UK, Block 9, Row 3, Grave 13	
	Ofw	PoW		
	Hptm	+	Cannock Chase/UK, Block 9, Row 3, Grave 13	
	Oblt	+	Cannock Chase/UK, Block 9, Row 3, Grave 13	
	Uffz			
	Uffz	Wounded		Hanke crew
	Oblt			
	Fw	Wounded		Wöhlermann crew
	Uffz	+	Ysselsteyn/Holland, Block BF, Row 4, Grave 78	Body washed ashore 20.09.1940
	Lt	+		
	Fw	+		

DORNIER Do 17 IN THE BATTLE OF BRITAIN

Date	Unit	Type	W/Nr	Codes	Name	Role
18.8.1940	8./KG 76	Do 17 Z			Szybinski, Hans	Beobachter
18.8.1940	8./KG 76	Do 17 Z			Ulbrich, Heinz	Bordschütze
18.8.1940	8./KG 76	Do 17 Z-2			Windschild, Werner	Flugzeugführer
18.8.1940	9./KG 76	Do 17 Z			Schümann, Max	Bordmechanike
18.8.1940	9./KG 76	Do 17 Z			Gaiser, Fritz	Bordmechanike
18.8.1940	9./KG 76	Do 17 Z			Malter, Erich	Bordfunker
18.8.1940	9./KG 76	Do 17 Z		F1+LT	Raab, Wilhelm	Flugzeugführer
18.8.1940	9./KG 76	Do 17 Z		F1+LT	Seuffert, Werner	Bordschütze
18.8.1940	9./KG 76	Do 17 Z		F1+LT	Wittmann, Erwin	Beobachter
18.8.1940	9./KG 76	Do 17 Z		F1+LT	Malter, Erich	Bordfunker
18.8.1940	9./KG 76	Do 17 Z			Maassen, Mathias	Flugzeugführer
18.8.1940	9./KG 76	Do 17 Z			Fretz, Peter	Bordmechanike
18.8.1940	9./KG 76	Do 17 Z		F1+JT	Illg, Wilhelm	Beobachter
18.8.1940	9./KG 76	Do 17 Z		F1+JT	Magin, Hermann	Flugzeugführer
18.8.1940	9./KG 76	Do 17 Z		F1+JT	Strahlendorf, Hans	Bordfunker
18.8.1940	9./KG 76	Do 17 Z		F1+JT	Henke, Willi	Borbmechanike
18.8.1940	9./KG 76	Do 17 Z		F1+JT	Hinze, Georg	Kr.Ber.
18.8.1940	9./KG 76	Do 17 Z-2		F1+DT	Eberhart, Hugo	Bordfunker
18.8.1940	9./KG 76	Do 17 Z-2		F1+DT	Geier, Valentin	Bordmechanike
18.8.1940	9./KG 76	Do 17 Z-2		F1+DT	Lamberty, Rudolf	Flugzeugführer
18.8.1940	9./KG 76	Do 17 Z-2		F1+DT	Peters, Gustav	Beobachter
18.8.1940	9./KG 76	Do 17 Z-2		F1+DT	Roth, Joachim	Beobachter
18.8.1940	9./KG 76	Do 17 Z-2		F1+HT	Ahrends, Hans-Siegfried	Beobachter
18.8.1940	9./KG 76	Do 17 Z-2		F1+HT	Dietz, Hans	Bordmechanike
18.8.1940	9./KG 76	Do 17 Z-2		F1+HT	Greulich, Karl	Bordfunker
18.8.1940	9./KG 76	Do 17 Z-2		F1+HT	Petersen, Johannes	Flugzeugführer
18.8.1940	9./KG 76	Do 17 Z-2		F1+HT	Sommer, Otto	Passenger

DORNIER Do 17 CREW CASUALTIES

Exec	Rank	Fate	Burial	Notes
	Uffz	+	Bourdon/France, Block 16, Row 12, Grave 433	
	Gefr	+	Bourdon/France, Block 13, Row 14, Grave 527	
	Uffz			
	Fw	Wounded		Maasen crew
	Fw	+	Bourdon/France, Block 25, Row 18, Grave 709	Schmacher crew
	Uffz			
	Fw			
	Gefr			
	Lt	Wounded		Raab crew
	Uffz			
	Uffz			
	Uffz	+		Stephani crew
	Ofw			
	Oblt	Wounded/+	Bourdon/France, Block 7, Row 17, Grave 350	
	Uffz			
	Fw			
	Sd.Fhr			
	Fw	PoW		
	Ofw	PoW		
	Oblt	PoW		
	Hptm	PoW		
St Kap	Hptm	PoW		
	Oblt	+	Cannock Chase/UK, Block 5, Row 3, Grave 66	
	Uffz	+	Cannock Chase/UK, Block 5, Row 3, Grave 68	
	Fw	+	Cannock Chase/UK, Block 5, Row 3, Grave 67	
	Fw	+	Cannock Chase/UK, Block 5, Row 3, Grave 69	
	Oberst	+	Cannock Chase/UK, Block 5, Row 3, Grave 70	From G.K.S. 3

Date	Unit	Type	W/Nr	Codes	Name	Role
18.8.1940	9./KG 76	Do 17 Z-2			Schumacher, Bernhard	Flugzeugführer
18.8.1940	9./KG 76	Do 17 Z-2			Unger, Günther	Flugzeugführer
18.8.1940	9./KG 76	Do 17 Z-2			Moritz, Karl	Bordmechaniker
18.8.1940	9./KG 76	Do 17 Z-2			Schwab, Nikolaus	Bordfunker
18.8.1940	9./KG 76	Do 17 Z-2			Stephani, Otto	Flugzeugführer
18.8.1940	9./KG 76	Do 17 Z-3		F1+CT	Haas, Albert	Bordmechaniker
18.8.1940	9./KG 76	Do 17 Z-3		F1+CT	Reichel, Adolf	Flugzeugführer
18.8.1940	9./KG 76	Do 17 Z-3		F1+CT	von Pebal, Rolf	Kr.Ber.
19.8.1940	7./KG 2	Do 17 Z		U5+DR	Aldenhoven, Karl	Hilfsbeobachter
19.8.1940	7./KG 2	Do 17 Z		U5+DR	Jung, Werner	Bordmechaniker
19.8.1940	7./KG 2	Do 17 Z		U5+DR	Mumb, Josef	Flugzeugführer
19.8.1940	7./KG 2	Do 17 Z		U5+DR	Schwindt, Franz	Bordfunker
20.8.1940	7./KG 2	Do 17 Z-3			Illing, Siegfried	Bordmechaniker
20.8.1940	7./KG 2	Do 17 Z-3			Krieger, Peter	Flugzeugführer
20.8.1940	7./KG 2	Do 17 Z-3			Schneider, Günter	Bordfunker
20.8.1940	7./KG 2	Do 17 Z-3			Winter, Karl	Beobachter
20.8.1940	9./KG 2	Do 17 Z-3			Lawnik, Ernst	Bordfunker
20.8.1940	9./KG 2	Do 17 Z-3			Schlüter, Fritz	Bordmechaniker
20.8.1940	9./KG 2	Do 17 Z-3			Vallbracht, Fritz	Hilfsbeobachter
20.8.1940	9./KG 2	Do 17 Z-3			Weiler, Franz	Flugzeugführer
20.8.1940	9./KG 3	Do 17 Z-3		5K+FT	Brehmer, Kurt	Bordfunker
20.8.1940	9./KG 3	Do 17 Z-3		5K+FT	Böke, Kurt	Hilfsbeobachter
20.8.1940	9./KG 3	Do 17 Z-3		5K+FT	Heinrich, Richard	Bordschütze
20.8.1940	9./KG 3	Do 17 Z-3		5K+FT	Rüdinger, Emil	Flugzeugführer
21.8.1940	2./KG 2	Do 17 Z-3		U5+FK	Ermecke, Heinz	Flugzeugführer
21.8.1940	2./KG 2	Do 17 Z-3		U5+FK	Hermsen, Heinz	Bordfunker
21.8.1940	2./KG 2	Do 17 Z-3		U5+FK	Rasche, Kurt	Kr.Ber.

DORNIER Do 17 CREW CASUALTIES

Exec	Rank	Fate	Burial	Notes
	Uffz			Rescued by Kriegsmarine
	Uffz			Rescued by Kriegsmarine
	Wounded			Unger crew
	Uffz	Wounded/+		Stephani crew. Died 21.08.1940
	Fw	Wounded		
	Uffz	Wounded		Reichel crew
	Fw			
	Sd.Führer			Kr.Ber.Komp. 4
	Fw	PoW		
	Gefr	PoW		
	Lt	PoW		
	Gefr	PoW		
	Uffz			
	Lt			
	Gefr	Wounded		
	Uffz			
	Gefr	Wounded		
	Fw			
	Fw	Wounded		
	Ofw			
	Fw	PoW		
	Fw	PoW		
	Gefr	PoW		
	Fw	+	Cannock Chase/UK, Block 1, Row 11, Grave 441	
	Lt	+	Cannock Chase/UK, Block 5, Row 14, Grave 317	
	Uffz	PoW		
	Sdfhr	PoW		Kr.Ber.Komp. (Mot) 3

DORNIER Do 17 IN THE BATTLE OF BRITAIN

Date	Unit	Type	W/Nr	Codes	Name	Role
21.8.1940	2./KG 2	Do 17 Z-3		U5+FK	Wulf, Götz-Dieter	Beobachter
21.8.1940	8./KG 2	Do 17 Z		U5+CS	Behnke, Hans	Hilfsbeobachter
21.8.1940	8./KG 2	Do 17 Z		U5+CS	Ksienzyk, Konrad	Flugzeugführer
21.8.1940	8./KG 2	Do 17 Z		U5+CS	Sollfrank, Johann	Bordfunker
21.8.1940	8./KG 2	Do 17 Z		U5+CS	Sterz, Heinz	Bordmechaniker
21.8.1940	4./KG 3	Do 17 Z-3			Kaschner, Helmut	Bordschütze
21.8.1940	4./KG 3	Do 17 Z-3			Kotulla, Erich	Hilfsbeobachter
21.8.1940	4./KG 3	Do 17 Z-3			Krüger, Hellmut	Beobachter
21.8.1940	4./KG 3	Do 17 Z-3			Stolle, Wilhelm	Flugzeugführer
21.8.1940	4./KG 3	Do 17 Z-3			Schlafer, Erich	Bordfunker
21.8.1940	4./KG 3	Do 17 Z-3			Skibitzki, Bruno	Bordschütze
21.8.1940	4./KG 3	Do 17 Z-3			Wiegand, Volkhard	Bordfunker
21.8.1940	4./KG 3	Do 17 Z-3			Zimmermann, Max	Flugzeugführer
21.8.1940	6./KG 3	Do 17 Z-2		5K+BP	Langer, Hans	Bordschütze
21.8.1940	6./KG 3	Do 17 Z-2		5K+BP	Ludwig, Kurt	Bordschütze
21.8.1940	6./KG 3	Do 17 Z-2		5K+BP	Paterrok, Franz	Bombenschütze
21.8.1940	6./KG 3	Do 17 Z-2		5K+BP	Pöllmann, Georg	Flugzeugführer
21.8.1940	6./KG 3	Do 17 Z-3		5K+AP	Lehmann, Helmut	Bordfunker
21.8.1940	6./KG 3	Do 17 Z-3		5K+AP	Loos, Wilhelm	Bordfunker
21.8.1940	6./KG 3	Do 17 Z-3		5K+AP	Matschoß, Ulrich	Beobachter
21.8.1940	6./KG 3	Do 17 Z-3		5K+AP	Schwartz, Herbert	Flugzeugführer
22.8.1940	1./KG 2	Do 17 Z		U5+LH	Cellarius, Fritz	Bordmechaniker
22.8.1940	1./KG 2	Do 17 Z		U5+LH	Fremke, Günter	Flugzeugführer

DORNIER Do 17 CREW CASUALTIES

Exec	Rank	Fate	Burial	Notes
	Uffz	PoW		
	Uffz	PoW		
	Lt	PoW		
	Gefr	PoW		
	Flg	PoW		
	Uffz	PoW/+	Great Bircham (St. Mary) Churchyard, Norfolk/UK, Block 2, Row 1, Grave 1	
	Ofw	+	Cannock Chase, Block 5, Row 10, Grave 229	Body washed ashore 22.08.1940
	Lt	+	Cannock Chase, Block 5, Row 4, Grave 79	Body washed ashore 22.08.1940
	Ofw	+	Cannock Chase, Block 5, Row 4, Grave 80	Body washed ashore 22.08.1940
	Gefr	+		
	Uffz	+	Great Bircham (St. Mary) Churchyard, Norfolk, Block 2, Row 1, Grave 2	Body washed ashore 09.09.1940
	Uffz	Missing		
	Fw	Missing		
	Gefr	PoW		
	Gefr	PoW		
	Uffz	PoW		
	Uffz	PoW		
	Uffz	+	Cannock Chase, Block 3, Row 6, Grave 182	
	Ofw	+	Cannock Chase/UK, Block 3, Row 6, Grave 181	
	Oblt	PoW		
St Kap	Oblt	PoW		
	Fw	+	Bourdon/France, Block 22, Row 6, Grave 208	
	Obfhr	+	Bourdon/France, Block 22, Row 6, Grave 207	

DORNIER Do 17 IN THE BATTLE OF BRITAIN

Date	Unit	Type	W/Nr	Codes	Name	Role
22.8.1940	1./KG 2	Do 17 Z		U5+LH	Groß, Hans	Bordfunker
22.8.1940	1./KG 2	Do 17 Z		U5+LH	von Winterfeld, Wilhelm	Beobachter
22.8.1940	Wekusta 26	Do 17			Seeliger, Werner	Meteorologe
23.8.1940	Stabsst./KG 2	Do 17 Z		U5+EA	Dietl, Albert	Bordfunker
23.8.1940	Stabsst./KG 2	Do 17 Z		U5+EA	Hellmers, Johann-Heinrich	Beobachter
23.8.1940	Stabsst./KG 2	Do 17 Z		U5+EA	Seidel, Paul	Bordmechaniker
23.8.1940	Stabsst./KG 2	Do 17 Z		U5+EA	Wagner, Günter	Flugzeugführer
25.8.1940	3./KG 76	Do 17 Z			Eppelmann, Wilhelm	Flugzeugführer
25.8.1940	3./KG 76	Do 17 Z			Liebmann, Franz	Bordfunker
26.8.1940	1./Kü.Fl.Gr. 606	Do 17 Z-3	2676	7T+GH	Blüthgen, Otto	Bordfunker
26.8.1940	1./Kü.Fl.Gr. 606	Do 17 Z-3	2676	7T+GH	Diedrich, Horst	Beobachter
26.8.1940	1./Kü.Fl.Gr. 606	Do 17 Z-3	2676	7T+GH	Homann, Heinz	Bordmechaniker
26.8.1940	1./Kü.Fl.Gr. 606	Do 17 Z-3	2676	7T+GH	Ziehn, Otto	Flugzeugführer
26.8.1940	1./KG 2	Do 17 Z			Assum, Martin	Bordfunker
26.8.1940	1./KG 2	Do 17 Z			Deckarm, Karl	Beobachter
26.8.1940	1./KG 2	Do 17 Z			Krüger, Willi	Bordmechaniker
26.8.1940	1./KG 2	Do 17 Z			Wolpers, Heinrich	Flugzeugführer
26.8.1940	2./KG 2	Do 17 Z			Dilger, Robert	Flugzeugführer
26.8.1940	2./KG 2	Do 17 Z-3	2425	U5+GK	Buhr, Helmut	Bordfunker
26.8.1940	2./KG 2	Do 17 Z-3	2425	U5+GK	Gutzmann, Martin	Beobachter

DORNIER Do 17 CREW CASUALTIES

Exec	Rank	Fate	Burial	Notes
	Obgfr	+	Bourdon/France, Block 22, Row 6, Grave 209	
	Hptm	+	VDK: Bourdon/France, Block 22, Row 6, Grave 206	
	Reg. Rat.a.K.	+	Bourdon/France, Block 8, Row 8, Grave 281	Baled out when pilot suffered high altitude sickness. Body washed ashore
	Fw	PoW		
t Kap	Oblt	PoW		
	Uffz	PoW		
	Ofw	PoW		
	Uffz	Wounded		Rescued by Seenotdienst
	Uffz	Wounded		Rescued by Seenotdienst
	Hgfr	+		
	Lt.z.S	+		
	Uffz	+		
	Uffz	Missing		
	Gefr	Wounded		
	Ofw	Wounded		
	Uffz	Wounded		
	Uffz			
	Fw	Wounded		
	Uffz	PoW		
Gr Kdr	Major	PoW		

DORNIER Do 17 IN THE BATTLE OF BRITAIN

Date	Unit	Type	W/Nr	Codes	Name	Role
26.8.1940	2./KG 2	Do 17 Z-3	2425	U5+GK	Hertel, Siegfried	Beobachter
26.8.1940	2./KG 2	Do 17 Z-3	2425	U5+GK	Schmelzer, Ambrosius	Flugzeugführer
26.8.1940	2./KG 2	Do 17 Z-3	2637	U5+LK	Föße, Hans	Flugzeugführer
26.8.1940	2./KG 2	Do 17 Z-3	2637	U5+LK	Lunghard, Theodor	Bordmechaniker
26.8.1940	2./KG 2	Do 17 Z-3	2637	U5+LK	Röder, Julius	Bombenschütze
26.8.1940	2./KG 2	Do 17 Z-3	2637	U5+LK	Schmidt, Eilert	Bordfunker
26.8.1940	3./KG 2	Do 17 Z-2			Buchholz, Gottfried	Flugzeugführer
26.8.1940	3./KG 2	Do 17 Z-2			Conrad, Carl	Beobachter
26.8.1940	7./KG 2	Do 17 Z-2		U5+TR	Illing, Siegfried	Bordmechaniker
26.8.1940	7./KG 2	Do 17 Z-2		U5+TR	Krieger, Peter	Flugzeugführer
26.8.1940	7./KG 2	Do 17 Z-2		U5+TR	Schneider, Günter	Bordfunker
26.8.1940	7./KG 2	Do 17 Z-2		U5+TR	Winter, Karl	Hilfsbeobachter
26.8.1940	7./KG 2	Do 17 Z-3	1207	U5+BR	Knorky, Friedrich	Flugzeugführer
26.8.1940	7./KG 2	Do 17 Z-3	1207	U5+BR	Schadt, Ludwig	Bordmechaniker
26.8.1940	7./KG 2	Do 17 Z-3	1207	U5+BR	Schäfer, Heinrich	Hilfsbeobachter
26.8.1940	7./KG 2	Do 17 Z-3	1207	U5+BR	Simon, Willy	Bordfunker
26.8.1940	7./KG 2	Do 17 Z-3		U5+LR	Dußmann, Rudolf	Bordmechaniker
26.8.1940	7./KG 2	Do 17 Z-3		U5+LR	Heidenreich, Karl-Heinz	Beobachter
26.8.1940	7./KG 2	Do 17 Z-3		U5+LR	Hohnstädter, Wilhelm	Bordfunker
26.8.1940	7./KG 2	Do 17 Z-3		U5+LR	Panczak, Johann	Flugzeugführer
26.8.1940	9./KG 2	Do 17 Z			Schettler, Kurt	Bordmechaniker
26.8.1940	2./KG 3	Do 17 Z-2	2541		Krause, Hermann	Bombenschütze
26.8.1940	2./KG 3	Do 17 Z-2	2541		Liedig, Adolf	Bordschütze
26.8.1940	2./KG 3	Do 17 Z-2	2541		Wiesnewski, Johann	Flugzeugführer
26.8.1940	7./KG 3	Do 17 Z	3329	5K+GR	Henning, Heinz	Bordfunker
26.8.1940	7./KG 3	Do 17 Z	3329	5K+GR	Oerter, Theodor	Bordmechaniker
26.8.1940	7./KG 3	Do 17 Z	3329	5K+GR	Pott, Karl	Bordschütze
26.8.1940	7./KG 3	Do 17 Z	3329	5K+GR	Sachse, Heinz	Flugzeugführer
26.8.1940	7./KG 3	Do 17 Z	3602		Päßler, Horst	Bombenschütze

DORNIER Do 17 CREW CASUALTIES

Exec	Rank	Fate	Burial	Notes
	Oblt	+	Cannock Chase/UK, Block 1, Row 11, Grave 440	
	Uffz	PoW		
	Hptm	PoW		
	Uffz	PoW		
	Obgfr	PoW		
	Uffz	PoW		
St Kap	Oblt	Wounded		
	Oblt	Wounded		
	Uffz	PoW		
	Lt	PoW		
	Gefr	PoW		
	Uffz	PoW		
	Uffz	PoW		
	Gefr	PoW		
	Uffz	PoW		
	Uffz	PoW		
	Uffz	PoW		
	Oblt	+	Saffron Walden Cemetery, Essex/UK, Block 41, Grave 1	
	Fw	PoW		
	Fw	PoW/+	Saffron Walden Cemetery, Essex/UK, Block 41, Grave 2	
	Fw	Wounded		
	Gefr	+	Lommel/Belgium, Block 49, Grave 177	
	Ogfr	Wounded		
	Lt	Wounded		
	Uffz	Wounded		
	Uffz	Wounded		
	Gefr	Wounded		
	Lt	+		
	Uffz	Wounded		

Date	Unit	Type	W/Nr	Codes	Name	Role
26.8.1940	7./KG 3	Do 17 Z-2	1160	5K+AR	Effmert, Willi	Flugzeugführer
26.8.1940	7./KG 3	Do 17 Z-2	1160	5K+AR	Huhn, Heinz	Bordschütze
26.8.1940	7./KG 3	Do 17 Z-2	1160	5K+AR	Reinhardt, Helmut	Bordfunker
26.8.1940	7./KG 3	Do 17 Z-2	1160	5K+AR	Ritzel, Hermann	Bombenschütze
26.8.1940	7./KG 3	Do 17 Z-3	2646	5K+ER	Eggert, Karl	Flugzeugführer
26.8.1940	7./KG 3	Do 17 Z-3	2646	5K+ER	Haupt, Rudolf	Bombenschütze
26.8.1940	7./KG 3	Do 17 Z-3	2646	5K+ER	Knochenmuß, Walter	Bordschütze
26.8.1940	7./KG 3	Do 17 Z-3	2646	5K+ER	Ramm, Kurt	Bordfunker
26.8.1940	7./KG 3	Do 17 Z-3	2822		Kniesburges, Konrad	Bordfunker
26.8.1940	7./KG 3	Do 17 Z-3	2822		Meyer, August	Bombenschütze
27.8.1940	3.(F)/31	Do 17 P		5D+JL	Haffa, Walter	
27.8.1940	3.(F)/31	Do 17 P		5D+JL	Klauschenke, Gustav	
27.8.1940	3.(F)/31	Do 17 P		5D+JL	Schlesiel, Johannes	
27.8.1940	5./KG 2	Do 17 Z-2	4188		Butz, Josef	Bordfunker
27.8.1940	5./KG 2	Do 17 Z-2	4188		Gohr, Harry	Bordmechaniker
27.8.1940	5./KG 2	Do 17 Z-2	4188		Petraschke, Helmut	Hilfsbeobachter
28.8.1940	2./Kü.Fl.Gr. 606	Do 17 Z		7T+DK	Hoser, Fritz	Flugzeugführer
28.8.1940	2./Kü.Fl.Gr. 606	Do 17 Z		7T+DK	Hundt, Herbert	Bordmechaniker
28.8.1940	2./Kü.Fl.Gr. 606	Do 17 Z		7T+DK	Theißen, Willi	Bordfunker
28.8.1940	2./Kü.Fl.Gr. 606	Do 17 Z		7T+DK	Waldecker, Helmut	Beobachter
28.8.1940	1./KG 3	Do 17 Z-3	2807	5K+JH	Fedder, Hans	Bordmechaniker
28.8.1940	1./KG 3	Do 17 Z-3	2807	5K+JH	Graf von Platen-Hallermund, Rudolf	Flugzeugführer
28.8.1940	1./KG 3	Do 17 Z-3	2807	5K+JH	Köhler, Hermann	Hilfsbeobachter
28.8.1940	1./KG 3	Do 17 Z-3	2807	5K+JH	Ohlsen, Kurt	Bordfunker
28.8.1940	3./KG 3	Do 17 Z-2	3378		Senk, Friedrich	Bombenschütze

DORNIER Do 17 CREW CASUALTIES

xec	Rank	Fate	Burial	Notes
	Fw	PoW		
	Gefr	+	Cannock Chase/UK, Block 1, Row 11, Grave 405	
	Uffz	+	Ysselsteyn/Holland, Block BQ, Row 6, Grave 136	
	Uffz	PoW		
	Lt	PoW/+	Margate Cemetery, Kent/UK, Block L, Grave 15033	
	Uffz	PoW		
	Obgfr	+	Margate Cemetery, Kent/UK, Block L, Grave 15032	Body washed ashore
	Obgfr	PoW		
	Ogfr	Wounded		
	Gefr	Wounded		
	Lt	PoW		
	Fw	PoW		
	Gefr	PoW		
	Uffz	Wounded		
	Uffz	Wounded		
	Fw	Wounded		
	Ofw			
	Uffz			
	Uffz	+		
	Uffz	Wounded		
	Oblt	+	Lommel/Belgium, Block 49, Grave 190	
	Fw	+	Lommel/Belgium, Block 49, Grave 183	
	Uffz	Wounded		
	Uffz	+	Schleiden-Gemünd/Eifel, Grave 394	

171

Date	Unit	Type	W/Nr	Codes	Name	Role
28.8.1940	3./KG 3	Do 17 Z-2	3378		Solf, Josef	Bordfunker
28.8.1940	3./KG 3	Do 17 Z-2	3378		Vogel, Reinhard	Bordschütze
28.8.1940	3./KG 3	Do 17 Z-2	3378		Zimmermann, Heinrich	Flugzeugführer
28.8.1940	6./KG 3	Do 17 Z-3	4251	5K+LP	Brückmann, Anton	Bombenschütze
28.8.1940	6./KG 3	Do 17 Z-3	4251	5K+LP	Burghardt, Artur	Bombenschütze
28.8.1940	6./KG 3	Do 17 Z-3	4251	5K+LP	Gailer, Willi	Bordfunker
28.8.1940	6./KG 3	Do 17 Z-3	4251	5K+LP	Krug, Peter	Flugzeugführer
29.8.1940	1./Kü.Fl.Gr. 606	Do 17 Z-3	2878	7T+GH	Hillmann, Wolfgang	Flugzeugführer
29.8.1940	1./Kü.Fl.Gr. 606	Do 17 Z-3	2878	7T+GH	Paul, Friedrich	Bordmechaniker
29.8.1940	1./Kü.Fl.Gr. 606	Do 17 Z-3	2878	7T+GH	Rees, Ernst	Beobachter
29.8.1940	1./Kü.Fl.Gr. 606	Do 17 Z-3	2878	7T+GH	Siedentopf, Kurt	Bordfunker
29.8.1940	6./KG 2	Do 17 Z-3	2839	U5+FP	Kindler, Alfred	Flugzeugführer
29.8.1940	6./KG 2	Do 17 Z-3	2839	U5+FP	Matussek, Horst	Bordfunker
29.8.1940	6./KG 2	Do 17 Z-3	2839	U5+FP	Spreter, Josef	Bordmechaniker
29.8.1940	6./KG 3	Do 17 Z-3	3480	5K+FP	Hein, Günther	Flugzeugführer
29.8.1940	6./KG 3	Do 17 Z-3	3480	5K+FP	Schubert, Gerhard	Bombenschütze
29.8.1940	6./KG 3	Do 17 Z-3	3480	5K+FP	Zein, Günther	Flugzeugführer
30.8.1940	3.(F)/22	Do 17 P	1119	4N+AL	Aigner, Anton	Beobachter
30.8.1940	3.(F)/22	Do 17 P	1119	4N+AL	Schobert, Andreas	Bordfunker
30.8.1940	3.(F)/22	Do 17 P	1119	4N+AL	von Seebeck, Gert	Flugzeugführer
30.8.1940	3./Kü.Fl.Gr. 606	Do 17 Z-3	2838	7T+GL	Hanschke, Helmut	Beobachter
30.8.1940	3./Kü.Fl.Gr. 606	Do 17 Z-3	2838	7T+GL	Hesse, Günter	Flugzeugführer

DORNIER Do 17 CREW CASUALTIES

Exec	Rank	Fate	Burial	Notes
	Fw	+	Schleiden-Gemünd/Eifel, Grave 384	
	Uffz	+	Schleiden-Gemünd/Eifel, Grave 357	
	Uffz	+	VDK: Schleiden-Gemünd/ Eufel, Grave 388	
	Flg	PoW		
	Gefr	PoW		
	Gefr	PoW		
	Lt	PoW		
	Uffz	+		
	Uffz	Missing		
	Lt.z.S	+		
	Uffz	Missing		
	Oblt			
	Uffz	+	Bourdon/France, Block 30, Row 15, Grave 565	
	Ofw	Wounded/+	Bourdon/France, Block 30, Row 14, Grave 554	
	Uffz	+	Lommel/Belgium, Block 41, Grave 533	
	Gefr	+	Lommel/Belgium, Block 41, Grave 534	
	Lt	+	VDK: Lommel/Belgium, Block 41, Grave 530	
	Fw	Missing		
	Uffz	Missing		
	Lt.z.S	Missing		
	Lt.z.S	+	Berneuil/France, Block 3, Row 16, Grave 838	
	Fw	+		

DORNIER Do 17 IN THE BATTLE OF BRITAIN

Date	Unit	Type	W/Nr	Codes	Name	Role
30.8.1940	3./Kü.Fl.Gr. 606	Do 17 Z-3	2838	7T+GL	Marschner, Hans	Bordfunker
30.8.1940	3./Kü.Fl.Gr. 606	Do 17 Z-3	2838	7T+GL	Meinicke, Hans	Bordmechaniker
30.8.1940	9./KG 2	Do 17 Z-3	2868	U5+FT	Heutz, Josef	Bordmechaniker
30.8.1940	9./KG 2	Do 17 Z-3	2868	U5+FT	Kübler, Karl	Hilfsbeobachter
30.8.1940	9./KG 2	Do 17 Z-3	2868	U5+FT	Oehme, Fritz	Bordfunker
30.8.1940	9./KG 2	Do 17 Z-3	2868	U5+FT	Wittmann, Anton	Flugzeugführer
31.8.1940	5./KG 2	Do 17 Z-3	3483	U5+CN	Kriegel, Martin	Beobachter
31.8.1940	5./KG 2	Do 17 Z-3	3483	U5+CN	Niegisch, Paul	Bordfunker
31.8.1940	5./KG 2	Do 17 Z-3	3483	U5+CN	Schildt, Heinz-Günther	Flugzeugführer
31.8.1940	5./KG 2	Do 17 Z-3	3483	U5+CN	Swientek, Emil	Bordmechaniker
31.8.1940	8./KG 2	Do 17 Z			Neumann, Günter	Bordmechaniker
31.8.1940	Stab III/ KG 2	Do 17 Z-2	3356	U5+AD	Fuchs, Adolf	Beobachter
31.8.1940	3./KG 3	Do 17 Z-2	1178	5K+KL	Hefter, Werner	Flugzeugführer
31.8.1940	3./KG 3	Do 17 Z-2	1178	5K+KL	Jahraus, Kurt	Bordschütze
31.8.1940	3./KG 3	Do 17 Z-2	1178	5K+KL	Prüsener, Joseph	Bombenschütze
31.8.1940	3./KG 3	Do 17 Z-2	1178	5K+KL	Schubert, Walter	Bordfunker
31.8.1940	3./KG 3	Do 17 Z-2	3299	5K+HL	Engel, Konrad	Bombenschütze
31.8.1940	3./KG 3	Do 17 Z-2	3299	5K+HL	Kleimeier, Walter	Flugzeugführer
31.8.1940	3./KG 3	Do 17 Z-2	3299	5K+HL	Zwiener, Emil	Bordfunker
31.8.1940	4./KG 3	Do 17 Z			Staake, Horst	Bordschütze
31.8.1940	4./KG 3	Do 17 Z			Hallmann, Adolf	Bordmechaniker
31.8.1940	4./KG 3	Do 17 Z-2	3264	5K+KM	Bock, Ernst	Bordfunker
31.8.1940	4./KG 3	Do 17 Z-2	3264	5K+KM	Bulach, Alfons	
31.8.1940	4./KG 3	Do 17 Z-2	3264	5K+KM	Gahrtz, Heinz	Beobachter
31.8.1940	4./KG 3	Do 17 Z-2	3264	5K+KM	Neumann, Ernst	Bordschütze
31.8.1940	4./KG 3	Do 17 Z-2	3456	5K+BC	Bobik, Hans	Bordfunker

DORNIER Do 17 CREW CASUALTIES

xec	Rank	Fate	Burial	Notes
	Uffz	+		
	Uffz	+		
	Uffz	Wounded		
	Gefr	+	Bourdon/France, Block 22, Row 6, Grave 216	
	Gefr	+	Bourdon/France, Block 22, Row 6, Grave 214	
	Lt	+	Bourdon/France, Block 22, Row 6, Grave 215	
	Fw			
	Gefr			
	Lt			
	Uffz	Wounded		
	Uffz	Wounded		
Gr Kdr	Major	Wounded		
	Uffz	Wounded		
	Gefr	Wounded		
	Fw	Wounded		
	Uffz	+	Lommel/Belgium, Block 49, Grave 188	
	Fw	Wounded		
	Fw	Wounded		
	Uffz	Wounded		
	Gefr	Wounded		
	Fw	Wounded		5./KG 3
	Uffz	PoW/+		
	Ofw	PoW		
	Oblt	PoW		
	Gefr	PoW		
	Gefr	+	Lommel/Belgium, Block 49, Grave 364	

DORNIER Do 17 IN THE BATTLE OF BRITAIN

Date	Unit	Type	W/Nr	Codes	Name	Role
31.8.1940	4./KG 3	Do 17 Z-2	3456	5K+BC	Kallek, Eduard	Bordschütze
31.8.1940	4./KG 3	Do 17 Z-2	3456	5K+BC	Ladda, Friedrich	Bombenschütze
31.8.1940	4./KG 3	Do 17 Z-2	3456	5K+BC	Schopper, Sieghart	Flugzeugführer
31.8.1940	4./KG 3	Do 17 Z-3	2669	5K+LM	Berndt, Hubert	Bordfunker
31.8.1940	4./KG 3	Do 17 Z-3	2669	5K+LM	Kostropetsch, Fritz	Bombenschütze
31.8.1940	4./KG 3	Do 17 Z-3	2669	5K+LM	Lange, Willi	Flugzeugführer
31.8.1940	4./KG 3	Do 17 Z-3	2669	5K+LM	Wünsch, Hans	Bordmechaniker
31.8.1940	5./KG 3	Do 17 Z-3	3414	5K+GN	Blasche, Herbert	Flugzeugführer
31.8.1940	5./KG 3	Do 17 Z-3	3414	5K+GN	Gudat, Emil	Bordfunker
31.8.1940	5./KG 3	Do 17 Z-3	3414	5K+GN	Nickl, Bruno	Hilfsbeobachter
31.8.1940	5./KG 3	Do 17 Z-3	3414	5K+GN	Sonntag, Walter	Bordmechaniker
31.8.1940	2./KG 76	Do 17 Z	3316	F1+BK	Bloß, Albert	Bordfunker
31.8.1940	2./KG 76	Do 17 Z	3316	F1+BK	Kleppmeier, Josef	Flugzeugführer
31.8.1940	2./KG 76	Do 17 Z	3316	F1+BK	Lang, Heinrich	Bordmechaniker
31.8.1940	2./KG 76	Do 17 Z	3316	F1+BK	Pfähler, Harald	Hilfsbeobachter
1.9.1940	2./KG 76	Do 17 Z			Schadhauser, Adalbert	Bordfunker
1.9.1940	9./KG 76	Do 17 Z	3369	F1+AT	Illg, Wilhelm	Beobachter
1.9.1940	9./KG 76	Do 17 Z	3369	F1+AT	Maaßen, Mathias	Flugzeugführer
1.9.1940	9./KG 76	Do 17 Z	3369	F1+AT	Spieß, Georg	Bordfunker
1.9.1940	9./KG 76	Do 17 Z	3369	F1+AT	Wöhner, Heinrich	Bordschütze
1.9.1940	9./KG 76	Do 17 Z			Hirsinger, Hermann	Bordmechaniker
2.9.1940	8./KG 3	Do 17 Z-2	1145	5K+MS	de Lalande, Jürgen	Beobachter
2.9.1940	9./KG 3	Do 17 Z-2	1187	5K+MT	Kindler, Karl	Bombenschütze
2.9.1940	9./KG 3	Do 17 Z-2	1187	5K+MT	Mai, Klaus	Bordschütze
2.9.1940	9./KG 3	Do 17 Z-2	1187	5K+MT	Riedel, Hans	Flugzeugführer
2.9.1940	9./KG 3	Do 17 Z-2	1187	5K+MT	Steinadler, Hans	Bordfunker
2.9.1940	9./KG 3	Do 17 Z-2	3269	5K+BT	Hilbrecht, Kurt	Bordfunker
2.9.1940	9./KG 3	Do 17 Z-2	3269	5K+BT	Rohr, Ulrich	Flugzeugführer
2.9.1940	9./KG 3	Do 17 Z-2	3269	5K+BT	Seidel, Karl	Bordmechaniker
2.9.1940	9./KG 3	Do 17 Z-2	3269	5K+BT	Sprink, Otto	Hilfsbeobachter

DORNIER Do 17 CREW CASUALTIES

xec	Rank	Fate	Burial	Notes
	Ogfr	Wounded		
	Uffz	Wounded		
	Lt	Wounded		
	Fw	PoW		
	Uffz	PoW		
	Ofw	PoW		
	Fw	PoW		
	Uffz	PoW		
	Fw	PoW		
	Fw	Missing		
	Uffz	PoW		
	Uffz	PoW		
	Lt	PoW		
	Obfhr	PoW		
	Fw	PoW		
	Uffz	Wounded		
	Ofw	PoW		
	Fw	PoW		
	Gefr	+	Hawkinge Cemetery, Kent/ UK, Block O, Grave 24	
	Fw	PoW		
	Uffz	Wounded		
	Hptm	Wounded		
	Gefr	Wounded		
Kr.Ber.	Lt	+	Bourdon/France, Block 16, Row 12, Grave 426	Lw.Kr.Ber.Kp. (mot) 3
	Uffz	Wounded		
	Ogfr	Wounded		
	Uffz	PoW/+	Cannock Chase/UK, Block 1, Grave 369	
	Oblt	PoW		
	Fw	PoW		
	Fw	PoW		

DORNIER Do 17 IN THE BATTLE OF BRITAIN

Date	Unit	Type	W/Nr	Codes	Name	Role
3.9.1940	5./KG 2	Do 17 Z-2	3450	U5+AN	Kriegel, Martin	Hilfsbeobachter
3.9.1940	5./KG 2	Do 17 Z-2	3450	U5+AN	Niegisch, Paul	Bordfunker
3.9.1940	5./KG 2	Do 17 Z-2	3450	U5+AN	Schildt, Heinz-Günther	Flugzeugführer
3.9.1940	5./KG 2	Do 17 Z-2	3450	U5+AN	Swientek, Emil	Bordmechaniker
5.9.1940	6./KG 2	Do 17 Z	2828	U5+KP	Herrmann, Anton	Flugzeugführer
5.9.1940	6./KG 2	Do 17 Z	2828	U5+KP	Hoffmann, Kurt	Bordschütze
5.9.1940	6./KG 2	Do 17 Z-2	1134	U5+FP	Jakowski, Willi	Bombenschütze
5.9.1940	6./KG 2	Do 17 Z-2	1134	U5+FP	Ziegans, Josef	Bordschütze
7.9.1940	4./KG 2	Do 17 Z	2830	U5+FM	Christoph, Paul	Flugzeugführer
7.9.1940	4./KG 2	Do 17 Z	2830	U5+FM	Greiner, Albert	Beobachter
7.9.1940	4./KG 2	Do 17 Z	2830	U5+FM	Pilz, Fritz	Bordschütze
7.9.1940	4./KG 2	Do 17 Z	2830	U5+FM	Treuer, Günther	Bordfunker
7.9.1940	9./KG 2	Do 17 Z			Haufe, Werner	Bordfunker
7.9.1940	Stabsst./KG 2	Do 17 Z	2674	U5+CA	Klausmann, Andreas	Bordmechaniker
7.9.1940	5./KG 3	Do 17 Z	2840	5K+FN	Kalz, Walter	Beobachter
7.9.1940	5./KG 3	Do 17 Z	2840	5K+FN	Leitner, Karl	Flugzeugführer
7.9.1940	8./KG 3	Do 17 Z			Duryn, Max	Bordmechaniker
7.9.1940	8./KG 3	Do 17 Z			Heigl, Heliodor	Bordfunker
7.9.1940	8./KG 3	Do 17 Z			Hennebruch, Wilhelm	Flugzeugführer
7.9.1940	9./KG 3	Do 17 Z			Riemann, Ferdinand	Bordmechaniker
7.9.1940	Stabsst./KG 3	Do 17 Z-3	2619	5K+DA	Huber, Ignaz	Bordmechaniker
7.9.1940	Stabsst./KG 3	Do 17 Z-3	2619	5K+DA	Kleine, Walter	Flugzeugführer
7.9.1940	Stabsst./KG 3	Do 17 Z-3	2619	5K+DA	Völkert, Ernst	Bordfunker
7.9.1940	Stabsst./KG 3	Do 17 Z-3	2619	5K+DA	Ötting, Friedrich	Beobachter
7.9.1940	Stabsst./KG 76	Do 17 Z	2596	F1+BA	Rosche, Erich	Bordfunker

DORNIER Do 17 CREW CASUALTIES

xec	Rank	Fate	Burial	Notes
	Fw	PoW		
	Gefr	+		
	Lt	+		
	Uffz	+		
	Fw			
	Gefr	Wounded		
	Flg	Wounded		
	Uffz	Wounded		
	Uffz	+	Bourdon/France, Block 8, Row 9, Grave 312	
	Uffz	+	Bourdon/France, Block 11, Row 14, Grave 515	
	Gefr	+	Bourdon/France, Block 17, Row 11, Grave 405	
	Uffz	+	Bourdon/France, Block 17, Row 11, Grave 400	
	Uffz	Wounded		
	Uffz	Wounded		
	Ofw	Wounded		
	Lt	Wounded		
	Uffz	Wounded		
	Ogfr	Wounded		
	Uffz	Wounded		
	Uffz	Wounded		
	Fw	Missing		
	Ofw	+	Ysselsteyn/Holland	Body washed ashore
	Uffz	Missing		
Kap	Hptm	+	Ysselsteyn/Holland, Block CL, Row 1, Grave 2	Body washed ashore at Bergen ann Zee 26.09.1940
	Fw	POW		

DORNIER Do 17 IN THE BATTLE OF BRITAIN

Date	Unit	Type	W/Nr	Codes	Name	Role
7.9.1940	Stabsst./KG 76	Do 17 Z	2596	F1+BA	Rupprecht, Walter	Bordschütze
7.9.1940	Stabsst./KG 76	Do 17 Z	2596	F1+BA	Schneider, Gottfried	Flugzeugführer
7.9.1940	Stabsst./KG 76	Do 17 Z	2596	F1+BA	Schneider, Karl	Hilfsbeobachter
8.9.1940	5./KG 2	Do 17 Z	3415	U5+LN	Flick, Heino	Bombenschütze
8.9.1940	5./KG 2	Do 17 Z	3415	U5+LN	Selter, Wilhelm	Bordschütze
8.9.1940	5./KG 2	Do 17 Z	3415	U5+LN	Trost, Wilhelm	Bordfunker
8.9.1940	5./KG 2	Do 17 Z	3415	U5+LN	Ziems, Martin	Flugzeugführer
8.9.1940	5./KG 2	Do 17 Z		U5+DN	Brendebach, Georg	Flugzeugführer
8.9.1940	5./KG 2	Do 17 Z		U5+DN	Hein, Albert	Beobachter
8.9.1940	5./KG 2	Do 17 Z		U5+DN	Lotz, Walter	Bordfunker
8.9.1940	5./KG 2	Do 17 Z		U5+DN	Steinhagen	Bordmechaniker
8.9.1940	5./KG 2	Do 17 Z-2	1130	U5+FN	Landenberger, Otto	Flugzeugführer
8.9.1940	5./KG 2	Do 17 Z-2	1130	U5+FN	Lotter, Friedrich	Beobachter
8.9.1940	5./KG 2	Do 17 Z-2	1130	U5+FN	Schütze, Paul	Bordschütze
8.9.1940	5./KG 2	Do 17 Z-2	1130	U5+FN	Strobel, Max	Bordfunker
8.9.1940	5./KG 2	Do 17 Z-3	2668	U5+BN	Hoffmann, Hans	Bordfunker
8.9.1940	5./KG 2	Do 17 Z-3	2668	U5+BN	Kohl, Willi	Bordschütze
8.9.1940	5./KG 2	Do 17 Z-3	2668	U5+BN	Schneider, Joachim	Flugzeugführer
8.9.1940	5./KG 2	Do 17 Z-3	2668	U5+BN	Schumacher, Josef	Beobachter
8.9.1940	3./KG 3	Do 17 Z-2	3321	5K+CL	Gaumnitz, Gottfried	Hilfsbeobachter
8.9.1940	3./KG 3	Do 17 Z-2	3321	5K+CL	Kückens, Rolf	Flugzeugführer
8.9.1940	3./KG 3	Do 17 Z-2	3321	5K+CL	Lehmann, Helmut	Bordschütze
10.9.1940	9./KG 76	Do 17 Z-3	2778	F1+ET	Domenig, Walter	Flugzeugführer

DORNIER Do 17 CREW CASUALTIES

xec	Rank	Fate	Burial	Notes
	Uffz	+	Cannock Chase/UK, Block 9, Row 4, Grave 21	
	Lt	+	Cannock Chase/UK, Block 9, Row 4, Grave 21	
	Ofw	+	Cannock Chase/UK, Block 9, Row 4, Grave 21	
	Uffz	Missing		
	Uffz	+	St.Margaret's Churchyard, Broomfield, UK	
	Uffz	0	St.Margaret's Churchyard, Broomfield, UK	
	Oblt	+	Maidstone Cemetery/UK, Block CCI, Grave 279	
	Fw			
	Lt			
	Fw			
	Fw			
	Lt	+	Cannock Chase/England, Block 9, Row 4, Grave 23	
	Gefr	+	Cannock Chase/England, Block 9, Row 4, Grave 23	
	Flg	+	Cannock Chase/England, Block 9, Row 4, Grave 23	
	Ofw	PoW		
	Ogefr	PoW		
	Flg	PoW		
	Oblt	PoW		
	Uffz	PoW		
	Lt	+	Lommel/Belgium, Block 49, Grave 182	
Kap	Hptm	+	Lommel/Belgium, Block 49, Grave 186	
	Fw	+	Lommel/Belgium, Block 49, Grave 184	
	Oblt	+	Cannock Chase/UK, Block 1, Row 3, Grave 102	

DORNIER Do 17 IN THE BATTLE OF BRITAIN

Date	Unit	Type	W/Nr	Codes	Name	Role
10.9.1940	9./KG 76	Do 17 Z-3	2778	F1+ET	Greza, Albert	Bordmechanik
10.9.1940	9./KG 76	Do 17 Z-3	2778	F1+ET	Nürnberg, Ernst	Bombenschütz
10.9.1940	9./KG 76	Do 17 Z-3	2778	F1+ET	Strahlendorf, Hans	Bordfunker
12.9.1940	4.(F)/121	Do 17 P	3530	7A+EM	Kühn, Hans	Bordmechanik
12.9.1940	4.(F)/121	Do 17 P	3530	7A+EM	Otto, Fritz	Flugzeugführer
14.9.1940	2./Kü.Fl.Gr. 606	Do 17 Z	2687	7T+FK	Kaiser, Willi	Bordmechanik
14.9.1940	2./Kü.Fl.Gr. 606	Do 17 Z	2687	7T+FK	Lindemann, Siegmund	Bordfunker
14.9.1940	2./Kü.Fl.Gr. 606	Do 17 Z	2687	7T+FK	Ose, Werner	Flugzeugführer
14.9.1940	2./Kü.Fl.Gr. 606	Do 17 Z	2687	7T+FK	Sibeth, Wilhelm	Beobachter
15.9.1940	5./KG 2	Do 17 Z			Rohr, Ludwig	Flugzeugführer
15.9.1940	5./KG 2	Do 17 Z-3	2304	U5+HN	Böhme, Gerhard	Flugzeugführer
15.9.1940	5./KG 2	Do 17 Z-3	2304	U5+HN	Huber, Georg	Bordfunker
15.9.1940	5./KG 2	Do 17 Z-3	2304	U5+HN	Irg, Franz	Bordschütze
15.9.1940	5./KG 2	Do 17 Z-3	2304	U5+HN	Möbius, Erich	Beobachter
15.9.1940	5./KG 2	Do 17 Z-3	2678	U5+CN	Haase, Kurt	Bordfunker
15.9.1940	5./KG 2	Do 17 Z-3	2678	U5+CN	Hafner, Willi	Beobachter
15.9.1940	5./KG 2	Do 17 Z-3	2678	U5+CN	Latz, Ulrich	Flugzeugführer
15.9.1940	5./KG 2	Do 17 Z-3	2678	U5+CN	Reinisch, Franz	Bordmechanik
15.9.1940	7./KG 2	Do 17 Z	2539	U5+ER	A	
15.9.1940	7./KG 2	Do 17 Z	2539	U5+ER	Moser, Edmund	Hilfsbeobachte
15.9.1940	7./KG 2	Do 17 Z	2539	U5+ER	Schwietring, Rolf	Flugzeugführer
15.9.1940	7./KG 2	Do 17 Z	2539	U5+ER	Slaby, Wilhelm	Bordfunker
15.9.1940	8./KG 2	Do 17 Z	2549	U5+FS	Flämig, Günter	Flugzeugführer
15.9.1940	8./KG 2	Do 17 Z	2549	U5+FS	Hirsch, Adolf	Hilfsbeobachte
15.9.1940	8./KG 2	Do 17 Z	2549	U5+FS	Sandmann, Clemens	Bordfunker
15.9.1940	8./KG 2	Do 17 Z	2549	U5+FS	Simon, Friedrich	Bordmechanik

DORNIER Do 17 CREW CASUALTIES

xec	Rank	Fate	Burial	Notes
	Gefr	PoW		
	Uffz	PoW		
	Uffz	+	Cannock Chase/UK, Block 1, Row 3, Grave 101	
	Uffz	+		
	Fw	+		
	Uffz	+		
	Uffz	Wounded		
	Uffz	+		
	Lt.z.S	+	Ploudaniel-Lesneven/France, Block 1, Row 2, Grave 47	
	Lt	Wounded		
	Uffz	+	Bourdon/France, Block 15, Row 12, Grave 447	Body washed ashore at Dunkirk 30.09.1940
	Uffz	+		
	Gefr	Missing		
	Uffz	Missing		
	Fw	PoW		
	Ofw	Missing		
	Oblt	PoW		
	Uffz	PoW		
		Wounded		
	Uffz	Wounded		
	Oblt	+	Bourdon/France, Block 22, Row 8, Grave 302	
	Gefr	Wounded		
	Uffz	Missing		
	Fw	Missing		
	Uffz	Missing		
	Fw	+		

Date	Unit	Type	W/Nr	Codes	Name	Role
15.9.1940	8./KG 2	Do 17 Z	3401	U5+DS	Ertl, Otto	Bordmechaniker
15.9.1940	8./KG 2	Do 17 Z	3401	U5+DS	Uerpmann, Karl	Bordfunker
15.9.1940	8./KG 2	Do 17 Z	3432	U5+JS	Steudel, Josef	Flugzeugführer
15.9.1940	8./KG 2	Do 17 Z	3432	U5+JS	Kleiber, Walter	Hilfsbeobachter
15.9.1940	8./KG 2	Do 17 Z	3432	U5+JS	Wachtel, Gotthardt	Bordfunker
15.9.1940	8./KG 2	Do 17 Z	3440	U5+PS	Kittmann, Werner	Beobachter
15.9.1940	8./KG 2	Do 17 Z	3440	U5+PS	Köhler, Wolfgang	Kr.Ber.
15.9.1940	8./KG 2	Do 17 Z	3440	U5+PS	Langer, Paul	Bordfunker
15.9.1940	8./KG 2	Do 17 Z	3440	U5+PS	Stampfer, Josef	Flugzeugführer
15.9.1940	8./KG 2	Do 17 Z	2644		Schenke, Wilhelm	Flugzeugführer
15.9.1940	8./KG 2	Do 17 Z	2644		Heinze, Gerhard	Hilfsbeobachter
15.9.1940	8./KG 2	Do 17 Z	2644		Sturm, Ludwig	Bordfunker
15.9.1940	8./KG 2	Do 17 Z	2644		Winkler, Fritz	Bordmechaniker
15.9.1940	8./KG 2	Do 17 Z-3	4242	U5+JR	Harjes, Hermann	Hilfsbeobachter
15.9.1940	8./KG 2	Do 17 Z-3	4242	U5+JR	Kalepky, Wolfgang	Flugzeugführer
15.9.1940	8./KG 2	Do 17 Z-3	4245	U5+GS	Holleck-Weithmann, Ingo	Beobachter
15.9.1940	8./KG 2	Do 17 Z-3	4245	U5+GS	Lessmann, Hubert	Flugzeugführer
15.9.1940	8./KG 2	Do 17 Z-3	4245	U5+GS	Lindemeier, Ernst	Bordmechaniker
15.9.1940	8./KG 2	Do 17 Z-3	4245	U5+GS	Schweighardt, Norbert	Bordfunker
15.9.1940	9./KG 2	Do 17 Z	3405	U5+FT	Hoffmann, Alfred	Bordmechaniker
15.9.1940	9./KG 2	Do 17 Z	3405	U5+FT	Hoppe, Hans	Bordfunker
15.9.1940	9./KG 2	Do 17 Z	3405	U5+FT	Staib, Karl-Oskar	Flugzeugführer
15.9.1940	9./KG 2	Do 17 Z	3405	U5+FT	Zierer, Josef	Hilfsbeobachter
15.9.1940	9./KG 2	Do 17 Z-2	3230	U5+ET	Glaser, Helmut	Hilfsbeobachter
15.9.1940	9./KG 2	Do 17 Z-2	3230	U5+ET	Krummheuer, Otto	Flugzeugführer
15.9.1940	9./KG 2	Do 17 Z-2	3230	U5+ET	Lenz, Richard	Bordmechaniker
15.9.1940	9./KG 2	Do 17 Z-2	3230	U5+ET	Sehrt, Jakob	Bordfunker

DORNIER Do 17 CREW CASUALTIES

Exec	Rank	Fate	Burial	Notes
	Gefr	+		
	Fw	+		
	Lt			
	Ofw	Wounded		
	Uffz			
	Oblt	PoW		
	Flg	PoW		Lw.Kr.Ber.Kp. (mot) 3
	Uffz	PoW		
	Uffz	PoW		
	Lt			
	Uffz	Wounded		
	Uffz	Wounded		
	Ofw	Wounded		
	Uffz	Wounded		
	Hptm	Wounded		
	Oblt	+		
	Hptm	Wounded		
	Uffz	Missing		
	Uffz	Wounded		
	Gefr	PoW		
	Uffz	+	Cannock Chase/UK, Block 1, Row 11, Grave 438	
	Obfhr	+	Cannock Chase/UK, Block 1, Grave 179	
	Gefr	PoW		
	Fw	+	Cannock Chase/UK, Block 1, Row 3, Grave 80	
	Uffz	+	Cannock Chase/UK, Block 1, Row 3, Grave 78	
	Uffz	+	Cannock Chase/UK, Block 4, Row 18, Grave 252	
	Uffz	PoW		

DORNIER Do 17 IN THE BATTLE OF BRITAIN

Date	Unit	Type	W/Nr	Codes	Name	Role
15.9.1940	Stabsst./ KG 2	Do 17 Z			Feßler, Willy	Bordfunker
15.9.1940	Stabsst./ KG 2	Do 17 Z			Rücker, Bringfried	Flugzeugführer
15.9.1940	4./KG 3	Do 17 Z-2	3294	5K+DM	Dümler, Kurt	Flugzeugführer
15.9.1940	4./KG 3	Do 17 Z-2	3294	5K+DM	Friebe, Gerhard	Bordschütze
15.9.1940	4./KG 3	Do 17 Z-2	3294	5K+DM	Maskolus, Horst	Bombenschütze
15.9.1940	4./KG 3	Do 17 Z-2	3294	5K+DM	Vogel, August	Bordfunker
15.9.1940	4./KG 3	Do 17 Z-2	3457	5K+JM	Burbulla, Wilhelm	Bordfunker
15.9.1940	4./KG 3	Do 17 Z-2	3457	5K+JM	Börmann, Hermann	Bordschütze
15.9.1940	4./KG 3	Do 17 Z-2	3457	5K+JM	Hausburg, Kurt	Bombenschütze
15.9.1940	4./KG 3	Do 17 Z-2	3457	5K+JM	Michaelis, Herbert	Flugzeugführer
15.9.1940	4./KG 3	Do 17 Z-3	2879	5K+AM	Granicky, Bernhard	Beobachter
15.9.1940	4./KG 3	Do 17 Z-3	2879	5K+AM	Gwidziel, Felix	Bordfunker
15.9.1940	4./KG 3	Do 17 Z-3	2879	5K+AM	Kirsch, Heinz	Bordmechaniker
15.9.1940	4./KG 3	Do 17 Z-3	2879	5K+AM	Schopper, Sieghart	Flugzeugführer
15.9.1940	4./KG 3	Do 17 Z-3	2881	5K+CM	Schild, Emil	Bordfunker
15.9.1940	4./KG 3	Do 17 Z-3	2881	5K+CM	Weymar, Helmut	Bordschütze
15.9.1940	4./KG 3	Do 17 Z-3	2881	5K+CM	Wien, Gerhard	Bombenschütze
15.9.1940	4./KG 3	Do 17 Z-3	2881	5K+CM	von Görtz, Manfred	Flugzeugführer
15.9.1940	5./KG 3	Do 17 Z-2	1176	5K+DN	Falke, Kurt	Bordfunker
15.9.1940	5./KG 3	Do 17 Z-2	1176	5K+DN	Franke, Willy	Bordmechaniker
15.9.1940	5./KG 3	Do 17 Z-2	1176	5K+DN	Langenhain, Adolf	Flugzeugführer
15.9.1940	5./KG 3	Do 17 Z-2	1176	5K+DN	Püttmann, Ernst	Beobachter
15.9.1940	5./KG 3	Do 17 Z-2	4200	5K+JN	Howind, Heinz	Hilfsbeobachter
15.9.1940	5./KG 3	Do 17 Z-2	4200	5K+JN	Höbel, Helmut	Bordmechaniker
15.9.1940	5./KG 3	Do 17 Z-2	4200	5K+JN	Rilling, Erich	Flugzeugführer
15.9.1940	5./KG 3	Do 17 Z-2	4200	5K+JN	Zimmermann, Eugen	Bordfunker

DORNIER Do 17 CREW CASUALTIES

xec	Rank	Fate	Burial	Notes
	Fw	Wounded		
	Fw	Wounded		
	Lt	+	Cannock Chase/UK, Block 1, Row 12, Grave 457	
	Uffz	PoW		
	Uffz	+	Cannock Chase/UK, Block 1, Grave 455	
	Fw	+	Cannock Chase/UK, Block 1, Row 12, Grave 453	
	Uffz	Wounded/+	Cannock Chase/UK, Block 5, Grave 51	
	Flg	PoW		
	Uffz	+	Cannock Chase/UK, Block 1, Row 7, Grave 247	
	Lt	PoW		
t Kap	Olt			
	Fw	Wounded		
	Fw	Wounded		
	Lt			
	Gefr	PoW		
	Gefr	PoW		
	Uffz	PoW		
	Fw	PoW		
	Fw	PoW		
	Fw	+	Cannock Chase/UK, Block 1, Grave 348	
	Oblt	Missing		
t Kap	Hptm	Missing		
	Ofw	PoW		
	Ofw	PoW		
	Ofw	+	Cannock Chase/UK, Block 1, Row 12, Grave 487	
	Fw	PoW		

DORNIER Do 17 IN THE BATTLE OF BRITAIN

Date	Unit	Type	W/Nr	Codes	Name	Role
15.9.1940	5./KG 3	Do 17 Z-3	2649	5K+HN	Kröhnert, Herbert	Bombenschütz
15.9.1940	5./KG 3	Do 17 Z-3	3458	5K+GN	Becker-Roß, Helmut	Beobachter
15.9.1940	5./KG 3	Do 17 Z-3	3458	5K+GN	Brinkmann, Wilhelm	Bordfunker
15.9.1940	5./KG 3	Do 17 Z-3	3458	5K+GN	Brückner, Georg	Bordmechanik
15.9.1940	5./KG 3	Do 17 Z-3	3458	5K+GN	Hansen, Alfred	Flugzeugführe
15.9.1940	6./KG 3	Do 17 Z-2	3470	5K+CP	Paschelke, Bruno	Bordfunker
15.9.1940	6./KG 3	Do 17 Z-3	4237	5K+EM	Harms-Ensink, Johann	Bordschütze
15.9.1940	1./KG 76	Do 17 Z	2361	F1+FH	Armbruster, Ludwig	Bordfunker
15.9.1940	1./KG 76	Do 17 Z	2361	F1+FH	Goschenhofer, Hans	Hilfsbeobachte
15.9.1940	1./KG 76	Do 17 Z	2361	F1+FH	Hammermeister, Leo	Bordmechanik
15.9.1940	1./KG 76	Do 17 Z	2361	F1+FH	Hubel, Gustav	Hilfsbeobachte
15.9.1940	1./KG 76	Do 17 Z	2361	F1+FH	Zehbe, Robert	Flugzeugführe
15.9.1940	1./KG 76	Do 17 Z	2364	F1+EH	Schmidt, Alfred	Bordmechanik
15.9.1940	1./KG 76	Do 17 Z	2364	F1+EH	Schwarz, Hugo	Bordmechanik
15.9.1940	1./KG 76	Do 17 Z	2364	F1+EH	Schätzle, Augustin	Bordfunker
15.9.1940	2./KG 76	Do 17 Z-2	2524	F1+JK	Figge, Hans	Flugzeugführe
15.9.1940	2./KG 76	Do 17 Z-2	2524	F1+JK	Florian, Martin	Beobachter
15.9.1940	2./KG 76	Do 17 Z-2	2524	F1+JK	Sommer, Friedrich	Bordmechanik
15.9.1940	2./KG 76	Do 17 Z-2	2524	F1+JK	Wagner, Karl	Bordfunker
15.9.1940	3./KG 76	Do 17 Z-3	2651	F1+FL	Niebler, Karl	Flugzeugführe
15.9.1940	3./KG 76	Do 17 Z-3	2651	F1+FL	Schatz, Hans	Bordmechanik
15.9.1940	3./KG 76	Do 17 Z-3	2651	F1+FL	Wilke, Karl-Ernst	Beobachter
15.9.1940	3./KG 76	Do 17 Z-3	2651	F1+FL	Wißmann, Karl	Bordmechanik
15.9.1940	3./KG 76	Do 17 Z-3	2651	F1+FL	Zrenner, Hans	Bordfunker

DORNIER Do 17 CREW CASUALTIES

xec	Rank	Fate	Burial	Notes
	Uffz	Wounded		
	Oblt	+	Bourdon/France, Block 7, Row 16, Grave 324	Body washed ashore
	Fw	+		
	Ofw	+		
	Fw	+		
	Uffz	+	Lommel/Belgium, Block 49, Grave 362	
	Flg	Wounded		
	Obgfr	PoW		
	Uffz	+	Cannock Chase/UK, Block 5, Grave 333	
	Uffz	PoW		
	Uffz	+	Cannock Chase/UK, Block 1, Row 4, Grave 132	
	Oblt	Wounded/+	Brookwood Military Cemetery, Surrey/UK, Block VI, Row L, Grave 4	
	Uffz	Wounded		
	Obgfr	Wounded		
	Uffz	+	Beauvais/France, Block 1, Row 2, Grave 58	
	Uffz			
	Oblt	Wounded		
	Ogfr			
	Uffz			
	Fw	+	Cannock Chase/UK, Block 1, Row 4, Grave 129	
	Uffz	+	Cannock Chase/UK, Block 1, Row 4, Grave 128	
	Oblt	PoW		
	Fw	+	Cannock Chase/UK, Block 1, Row 4, Grave 127	
	Fw	PoW		

Date	Unit	Type	W/Nr	Codes	Name	Role
15.9.1940	8./KG 76	Do 17 Z	2555	F1+FS	Heitsch, Rolf	Flugzeugführer
15.9.1940	8./KG 76	Do 17 Z	2555	F1+FS	Pfeiffer, Hans	Beobachter
15.9.1940	8./KG 76	Do 17 Z	2555	F1+FS	Sauter, Martin	Bordmechaniker
15.9.1940	8./KG 76	Do 17 Z	2555	F1+FS	Schmid, Stefan	Bordfunker
15.9.1940	8./KG 76	Do 17 Z-2	2578	F1+BS	Heitmann, Heinz	Bordmechaniker
15.9.1940	8./KG 76	Do 17 Z-2	2578	F1+BS	Keck, Lorenz	Flugzeugführer
15.9.1940	8./KG 76	Do 17 Z-2	2578	F1+BS	Rosenow, Günter	Bordfunker
15.9.1940	8./KG 76	Do 17 Z-2	2578	F1+BS	Zahn, Otto	Beobachter
15.9.1940	9./KG 76	Do 17 Z	2814	F1+AT	Böhme, Kurt	Bombenschütze
15.9.1940	9./KG 76	Do 17 Z	2814	F1+AT	Holdenried, Peter	Bordfunker
15.9.1940	9./KG 76	Do 17 Z	2814	F1+AT	Kotouc, Hans	Bordschütze
15.9.1940	9./KG 76	Do 17 Z	2814	F1+AT	Wagner, Anton	Flugzeugführer
15.9.1940	9./KG 76	Do 17 Z-2	3322	F1+DT	Malter, Erich	Bordfunker
15.9.1940	9./KG 76	Do 17 Z-2	3322	F1+DT	Raab, Wilhelm	Flugzeugführer
15.9.1940	9./KG 76	Do 17 Z-2	3322	F1+DT	Seuffert, Walter	Bordmechaniker
15.9.1940	9./KG 76	Do 17 Z-2	3322	F1+DT	Streit, Horst	Beobachter
19.9.1940	2./KG 3	Do 17 Z-2	3429	5K+LK	Geisler, Richard	Beobachter
19.9.1940	2./KG 3	Do 17 Z-2	3429	5K+LK	Schöneberg, Hans-Georg	Bordschütze
19.9.1940	6./KG 3	Do 17 Z-2	2535	5K+BP	Mergard, Ludwig	Flugzeugführer
19.9.1940	6./KG 3	Do 17 Z-2	2535	5K+BP	Scheuch, Friedrich	Bordschütze
21.9.1940	3./Kü.Fl.Gr. 606	Do 17 Z	3471	7T+CL	Simon, Bruno	Bordmechaniker
21.9.1940	3./Kü.Fl.Gr. 606	Do 17 Z	3471	7T+CL	von Bock und Polach, Otto	Flugzeugführer

xec	Rank	Fate	Burial	Notes
	Fw	PoW		
	Fw	PoW		
	Fw	PoW		
	Fw	+	Cannock Chase/UK, Block 1, Row 7, Grave 250	
	Fw	Missing		
	Fw	+	Cannock Chase/UK, Row 11, Grave 416	Body washed ashore 29.09.1940
	Uffz	+	Cannock Chase/UK, Block 1, Grave 309	Body washed ashore 15.10.1940
	Uffz	Missing		
	Ogefr	+	Cannock Chase/UK, Block 1, Row 5, Grave 143	
	Gefr	+	Cannock Chase/UK, Block 1, Row 5, Grave 145	
	Gefr	+	Cannock Chase/UK, Block 1, Row 5, Grave 144	
	Obfhr	+	Cannock Chase/UK, Block 1, Row 5, Grave 142	
	Uffz	+	Cannock Chase/UK, Block 1, Row 5, Grave 165	
	Fw	PoW		
	Fw	PoW		
	Ofw	PoW		
	Oblt	Wounded		
	Uffz	Wounded		
	Fw	Wounded		
	Ogfr	Wounded		
	Uffz	+		
	Uffz	+	Ploudaniel-Lesneven/ Frankreich, Block 1, Row 2, Grave 31	

DORNIER Do 17 IN THE BATTLE OF BRITAIN

Date	Unit	Type	W/Nr	Codes	Name	Role
21.9.1940	3./Kü.Fl.Gr. 606	Do 17 Z	3471	7T+CL	von Krosigk, Eberhard	Beobachter
21.9.1940	5./KG 2	Do 17 Z-2	3454	U5+FN	Kleiber, Walter	Beobachter
24.9.1940	1./KG 3	Do 17 Z-3	2633	5K+JH	Reichenbach, Alfred	Flugzeugführer
24.9.1940	2./KG 76	Do 17 Z	3317	F1+GK	Curth, Gottfried	Bordmechaniker
26.9.1940	Stabsst./ KG 3	Do 17 Z-3	2591	5K+FA	Siegmund, Walter	Bordmechaniker
27.9.1940	8./KG 2	Do 17 Z	2871	U5+ES	Kühn, Konrad	Bordmechaniker
27.9.1940	8./KG 2	Do 17 Z	2871	U5+ES	Langhorst, Heinz	Flugzeugführer
27.9.1940	8./KG 2	Do 17 Z	2871	U5+ES	Trautner, Erich	Beobachter
27.9.1940	8./KG 2	Do 17 Z	2871	U5+ES	Trost, Herbert	Bordfunker
28.9.1940	4./KG 2	Do 17 Z			Borner, Werner	Bordfunker
28.9.1940	4./KG 2	Do 17 Z			Genzow, Joachim	Flugzeugführer
28.9.1940	4./KG 2	Do 17 Z			Krüger, Berthold	Beobachter
28.9.1940	4./KG 2	Do 17 Z			Speer, Erich	Bordmechaniker
28.9.1940	5./KG 2	Do 17 Z	3355	U5+AN	Brandes, Robert	Beobachter
28.9.1940	5./KG 2	Do 17 Z	3355	U5+AN	Olbrich, Kurt	Bordfunker
28.9.1940	5./KG 2	Do 17 Z	3355	U5+AN	Peller, Karl	Bordmechaniker
28.9.1940	5./KG 2	Do 17 Z	3355	U5+AN	Roch, Hubert	Flugzeugführer
29.9.1940	4.(F)/14	Do 17 P	1096		Breitenbach, Georg	Beobachter
29.9.1940	4.(F)/14	Do 17 P	1096		Jordan, Werner	Bordfunker
29.9.1940	4.(F)/14	Do 17 P	1096		von Niessen, Bernhard	Flugzeugführer
30.9.1940	8./KG 2	Do 17 Z	2861	U5+BS	Klinkert, Walter	Bordfunker
30.9.1940	8./KG 2	Do 17 Z	2861	U5+BS	Koller, Peter	Beobachter

xec	Rank	Fate	Burial	Notes
	Oblt.z.S.	+	Ploudaniel-Lesneven/ Frankreich, Block 1, Row 2, Grave 32	
	Ofw	Wounded		
	Fw	Wounded		
	Uffz	Wounded		
	Fw	Wounded		
	Fw	+	Bourdon/France, Block 22, Row 9, Grave 351	
	Lt	+	Bourdon/France, Block 22, Row 9, Grave 352	
	Obgfr	+	Bourdon/France, Block 22, Row 9, Grave 350	
	Gefr	+	Bourdon/France, Block 22, Row 9, Grave 349	
	Ofw			
	Oblt			
	Ofw			
	Fw			
	Ofw	+	Bourdon/France, Block 6, Row 2, Grave 58	
	Obgfr	+	Bourdon/France, Block 6, Row 2, Grave 59	
	Gefr	+	Bourdon/France, Block 6, Row 2, Grave 60	
	Oblt	+	Bourdon/France, Block 6, Row 2, Grave 57	
	Lt	+	La Cambe/Frankreich, Block 36, Grave 111	
	Uffz	+		
	Lt	+	VDK: La Cambe/Frankreich, Block 36, Grave 109	
	Uffz	+	Bourdon/France, Block 22, Row 10, Grave 366	
	Uffz	+	Bourdon/France, Block 22, Row 10, Grave 367	

DORNIER Do 17 IN THE BATTLE OF BRITAIN

Date	Unit	Type	W/Nr	Codes	Name	Role
30.9.1940	8./KG 2	Do 17 Z	2861	U5+BS	Scheffel, Günter	Flugzeugführer
30.9.1940	8./KG 2	Do 17 Z	2861	U5+BS	Steigemann, Karl	Bordmechanike
30.9.1940	8./KG 3	Do 17 Z-3	4227	5K+HR	Bauer, Otto	Hilfsbeobachter
30.9.1940	8./KG 3	Do 17 Z-3	4227	5K+HR	Salomo, Alfred	Bordmechanike
30.9.1940	8./KG 3	Do 17 Z-3	4227	5K+HR	Schirling, Rudolf	Flugzeugführer
30.9.1940	8./KG 3	Do 17 Z-3	4227	5K+HR	Schroff, Ludwig	Bordfunker
1.10.1940	1./KG 2	Do 17 Z-2	1177	U5+BH	Ludzinski, Johann	Bordmechanike
1.10.1940	1./KG 2	Do 17 Z-2	1177	U5+BH	Stöckel, Ernst	Flugzeugführer
2.10.1940	Stabsst./ KG 2	Do 17 Z	3423	U5+FA	Bellmann, Hellmut	Bordmechanike
2.10.1940	Stabsst./ KG 2	Do 17 Z	3423	U5+FA	Eitze, Erich	Beobachter
2.10.1940	Stabsst./ KG 2	Do 17 Z	3423	U5+FA	Langer, Hans	Flugzeugführer
2.10.1940	Stabsst./ KG 2	Do 17 Z	3423	U5+FA	Seidel, Robert	Bordfunker
2.10.1940	9./KG 3	Do 17 Z-2	3270	5K+CT	Behnsch, Georg	Bordfunker
2.10.1940	9./KG 3	Do 17 Z-2	3270	5K+CT	Frangenheim, Wilhelm	Bombenschütze
2.10.1940	9./KG 3	Do 17 Z-2	3270	5K+CT	Müller, Reinhold	Bordmechanike
2.10.1940	9./KG 3	Do 17 Z-2	3270	5K+CT	Schulze, Rudolf	Flugzeugführer
2.10.1940	9./KG 77	Do 17 U	2427	3Z+FD	Below, Walter	Passenger
2.10.1940	9./KG 77	Do 17 U	2427	3Z+FD	Bierler, Georg	Bordfunker
2.10.1940	9./KG 77	Do 17 U	2427	3Z+FD	Hanke, Hubertus	Flugzeugführer
2.10.1940	9./KG 77	Do 17 U	2427	3Z+FD	Köhler, Walter	Passenger
2.10.1940	9./KG 77	Do 17 U	2427	3Z+FD	Schellhorn, Erwin	1.Wart
2.10.1940	9./KG 77	Do 17 U	2427	3Z+FD	Schäfer, Emil	Bombenschütze

DORNIER Do 17 CREW CASUALTIES

Exec	Rank	Fate	Burial	Notes
	Lt	+	Bourdon/France, Block 22, Row 10, Grave 368	
	Uffz	+	Bourdon/France, Block 22, Row 10, Grave 365	
	Fw	Missing		
	Fw	+	Cannock Chase/England, Block 5, Row 7, Grave 149	Body washed ashore 31.10.1940
	Fw	Missing		
	Uffz	Missing		
	Fw	+		
	Gefr	+	Bourdon/France, Block 22, Row 10, Grave 370	
	Uffz	PoW		
	Oblt	PoW		
t Kap	Oblt	PoW		
	Uffz	PoW		
	Gefr	+	Lommel/Belgium, Block 21, Grave 309	
	Fw	+	Lommel/Belgium, Block 21, Grave 121	
	Uffz	+	Lommel/Belgium, Block 21, Grave 132	
	Lt	+	Lommel/Belgium, Block 21, Grave 145	
	Ogfr	+		Stab/ KG 77
	Ogfr	+		
	Fw	+		
	Gefr	+		5.F.B.K./KG 77
	Uffz	+		
	Uffz	+		

Date	Unit	Type	W/Nr	Codes	Name	Role
3.10.1940	3./Kü.Fl.Gr. 606	Do 17 Z	3491	7T+EL	Dorfschmid, Josef	Bordmechaniker
3.10.1940	3./Kü.Fl.Gr. 606	Do 17 Z	3491	7T+EL	Schmid, Max-Dieter	Beobachter
3.10.1940	3./Kü.Fl.Gr. 606	Do 17 Z	3491	7T+EL	Seidenzahl, Rudolf	Bordfunker
3.10.1940	3./Kü.Fl.Gr. 606	Do 17 Z	3491	7T+EL	Wilms, Josef	Flugzeugführer
3.10.1940	2./KG 2	Do 17 Z-3	2638	U5+AK	Batschko, Herbert	Beobachter
3.10.1940	2./KG 2	Do 17 Z-3	2638	U5+AK	Conrau, Willi	
3.10.1940	2./KG 2	Do 17 Z-3	2638	U5+AK	Rederer, Josef	Flugzeugführer
3.10.1940	Wekusta 1 Ob.d.L.	Do 17 Z-2	2547	T5+IU	Heinrich, Rudolf	Meteorologe
3.10.1940	Wekusta 1 Ob.d.L.	Do 17 Z-2	2547	T5+IU	Meinecke	Flugzeugführer
3.10.1940	Wekusta 1 Ob.d.L.	Do 17 Z-2	2547	T5+IU	Wachsmuth, Horst	Bordwart
3.10.1940	Wekusta 1 Ob.d.L.	Do 17 Z-2	2547	T5+IU	Wohlfart, Joseph	Bordfunker
4.10.1940	1./Kü.Fl.Gr. 606	Do 17 Z			Ebert, Jürgen	Beobachter
4.10.1940	1./Kü.Fl.Gr. 606	Do 17 Z-3	3617	7T+CH	David, Paul	Flugzeugführer
4.10.1940	1./Kü.Fl.Gr. 606	Do 17 Z-3	3617	7T+CH	Fuchs, Kurt	Bordmechaniker
4.10.1940	1./Kü.Fl.Gr. 606	Do 17 Z-3	3617	7T+CH	Vollbrecht, Paul	Beobachter
4.10.1940	1./Kü.Fl.Gr. 606	Do 17 Z-3	3617	7T+CH	von Postel, Willi	Bordfunker
4.10.1940	1./KG 2	Do 17 Z-2	1212	U5+GH	Laub, Karl	Flugzeugführer
4.10.1940	5./KG 3	Do 17 Z-2	3343	5K+KN	Großmann, Rudolf	Bordmechaniker
4.10.1940	5./KG 3	Do 17 Z-2	3343	5K+KN	Kralemann, Friedrich	Flugzeugführer
4.10.1940	5./KG 3	Do 17 Z-2	3343	5K+KN	Meyer, Erich	Prüfer

DORNIER Do 17 CREW CASUALTIES

Exec	Rank	Fate	Burial	Notes
	Hgfr	+	Cannock Chase/UK, Block 5, Row 12, Grave 267	Body washed ashore 05.10.1940
	Lt.z.S	+	Cannock Chase/UK, Block 5, Grave 269	Body washed ashore 02.11.1940
	Uffz	Missing		
	Fw	Missing		
	Ofw	+	Bourdon/France, Block 22, Row 10, Grave 371	
	Fw	Wounded		
	Ofw	Wounded		
	Reg.Rat	Wounded/+		
	Fw			
	Fw			
	Fw			
	Lt.z.S	Wounded		
	Uffz	Missing		
	Uffz	+		
	Oblt.z.S	Missing		
	Uffz	Missing		
	Uffz	Wounded	Cannock Chase/UK, Block 9, Row 2, Grave 7	
	Uffz	Wounded		
	Fw	Wounded		
	Prüfmeister	+	Ysselsteyn/Holland, Block BA, Row 4, Grave 90	

DORNIER Do 17 IN THE BATTLE OF BRITAIN

Date	Unit	Type	W/Nr	Codes	Name	Role
4.10.1940	5./KG 3	Do 17 Z-2	3343	5K+KN	Meyer, Hans	Prüfer
4.10.1940	5./KG 3	Do 17 Z-2	3343	5K+KN	Scheidewig, Herbert	1.Wart
4.10.1940	7./KG 76	Do 17 Z-2	1136	F1+KR	Altenmüller, Rolf	Beobachter
4.10.1940	7./KG 76	Do 17 Z-2	1136	F1+KR	Hoffmann, Hermann	Bordmechaniker
4.10.1940	7./KG 76	Do 17 Z-2	1136	F1+KR	Schmelzle, Fritz	Bordfunker
4.10.1940	7./KG 76	Do 17 Z-2	1136	F1+KR	Zankl, Rudolf	Flugzeugführer
4.10.1940	9./KG 76	Do 17 Z	2888	F1+DT	Goldschmidt, Hermann	Bordfunker
4.10.1940	9./KG 76	Do 17 Z	2888	F1+DT	Meister, Karl-Günter	Flugzeugführer
4.10.1940	9./KG 76	Do 17 Z	2888	F1+DT	Waak, Oskar	Hilfsbeobachter
4.10.1940	9./KG 76	Do 17 Z	2888	F1+DT	Willer, Kurt	Bordmechaniker
6.10.1940	10./KG 2	Do 17 Z	2664	U5+AZ	Obermayer	Flugzeugführer
6.10.1940	2./KG 3	Do 17 Z-2	2537	5K+AK	Berghahn, Ernst	Flugzeugführer
6.10.1940	2./KG 3	Do 17 Z-2	2537	5K+AK	Dankenbring, Erich	Bombenschütze
6.10.1940	2./KG 3	Do 17 Z-2	2537	5K+AK	Scheibeler, Heinrich	Bordfunker
6.10.1940	2./KG 3	Do 17 Z-2	2537	5K+AK	Wellmann, Theodor	Bordschütze
6.10.1940	7./KG 76	Do 17 Z-3	4221	F1+FR	Morr, Friedrich	Flugzeugführer
6.10.1940	7./KG 76	Do 17 Z-3	4221	F1+FR	Mrozinski, Franz	Bordfunker
6.10.1940	7./KG 76	Do 17 Z-3	4221	F1+FR	Poh, Rudolf	Bordmechaniker
6.10.1940	7./KG 76	Do 17 Z-3	4221	F1+FR	Wagner, Hans	Hilfsbeobachter
7.10.1940	4.(F)/11	Do 17 P-1	3527	6M+HM	Fischer, Ekkehard	Beobachter
7.10.1940	4.(F)/11	Do 17 P-1	3527	6M+HM	Lier, Erich-Wolfgang	Flugzeugführer
7.10.1940	4.(F)/11	Do 17 P-1	3527	6M+HM	Müller, Richard	Bordfunker
8.10.1940	2.(F)/22	Do 17 P	3576	4N+GK	Freund, Hubert	Bordfunker
8.10.1940	2.(F)/22	Do 17 P	3576	4N+GK	Hardt, Konrad	Beobachter

DORNIER Do 17 CREW CASUALTIES

xec	Rank	Fate	Burial	Notes
	Prüfmeister	Wounded		
	Uffz	Wounded		
	Oblt	+	Champigny-St.Andre/France, Block 17, Grave 271	
	Uffz	+	Champigny-St.Andre/France, Block 17, Grave 274	
	Uffz	+	Champigny-St.Andre/France, Block 17, Grave 270	
	Ofw	+	Champigny-St.Andre/France, Block 17, Grave 272	
	Gefr	Wounded		
	Lt	+	Champigny-St.Andre/France, Block 17, Grave 273	
	Ofw	Wounded		
	Uffz	Wounded		
	Lt	Wounded		
	Lt	+	Lommel/Belgium, Block 49, Grave 179	
	Uffz	+	Lommel/Belgium, Block 48, Grave 200	
	Gefr	+	Lommel/Belgium, Block 48, Grave 476	
	Ogfr	+	Lommel/Belgium, Block 49, Grave 192	
	Lt	PoW		
	Uffz	PoW		
	Fw	PoW		
	Uffz	+	Cannock Chase/UK, Block 1, Row 1, Grave 1	
	Fw	+		
		Wounded		
	Uffz	Wounded		
	Ofw	PoW		
	Hptm	PoW		

Date	Unit	Type	W/Nr	Codes	Name	Role
8.10.1940	2.(F)/22	Do 17 P	3576	4N+GK	von Eickstedt, Egon	Flugzeugführer
9.10.1940	3./Kü.Fl.Gr. 606	Do 17 Z-3	2771	7T+HL	Göhlich, Kurt	Bordmechaniker
9.10.1940	3./Kü.Fl.Gr. 606	Do 17 Z-3	2771	7T+HL	Langer, Hans-Georg	Flugzeugführer
9.10.1940	3./Kü.Fl.Gr. 606	Do 17 Z-3	2771	7T+HL	Rübesam, Herbert	Bordfunker
9.10.1940	3./Kü.Fl.Gr. 606	Do 17 Z-3	2771	7T+HL	von Harbou, Erik	Beobachter
10.10.1940	1./KG 2	Do 17 Z	3442	U5+CH	Dilcher, Walter	Beobachter
10.10.1940	7./KG 3	Do 17 Z	3293	5K+AR	Weuster, Wilhelm	Bordschütze
11.10.1940	1./Kü.Fl.Gr. 606	Do 17 Z-3	2772	7T+EH	Arpert, Heinrich	Bordmechaniker
11.10.1940	1./Kü.Fl.Gr. 606	Do 17 Z-3	2772	7T+EH	Sudermann, Helmut	Bordfunker
11.10.1940	1./Kü.Fl.Gr. 606	Do 17 Z-3	2772	7T+EH	Vetterl, Josef	Flugzeugführer
11.10.1940	1./Kü.Fl.Gr. 606	Do 17 Z-3	2772	7T+EH	von Krause, Jürgen	Beobachter
11.10.1940	1./Kü.Fl.Gr. 606	Do 17 Z-5	2787	7T+HH	Hagen, Wilhelm	Flugzeugführer
11.10.1940	1./Kü.Fl.Gr. 606	Do 17 Z-5	2787	7T+HH	Heine, Karl-Franz	Beobachter
11.10.1940	1./Kü.Fl.Gr. 606	Do 17 Z-5	2787	7T+HH	Johannsen, Heinz	Bordmechaniker
11.10.1940	1./Kü.Fl.Gr. 606	Do 17 Z-5	2787	7T+HH	Staas, Hans	Bordfunker
11.10.1940	2./Kü.Fl.Gr. 606	Do 17 Z-3	3475	7T+EK	Felber, Horst	Beobachter
11.10.1940	2./Kü.Fl.Gr. 606	Do 17 Z-3	3475	7T+EK	Hoppmann, Walter	Bordfunker
11.10.1940	2./Kü.Fl.Gr. 606	Do 17 Z-3	3475	7T+EK	Richter, Friedrich-Wilhelm	Flugzeugführer

DORNIER Do 17 CREW CASUALTIES

Exec	Rank	Fate	Burial	Notes
	Lt	PoW		
	Fw	+	Cannock Chase/UK, Block 5, Grave 268	
	Fw	+		
	Ogefr	+		
	Lt.z.S	+		
	Lt	+	Bourdon/France, Block 22, Row 11, Grave 402	
	Gefr	Wounded		
	Fw	PoW		
	Ogefr	PoW		
	Fw	Missing		
	Lt.z.S	PoW		
	Ofw			
	Olt.z.S.			
	Uffz	+	Cannock Chase/UK, Block 7, Row 8, Grave 191	
	Fw	PoW		
	Lt.z.S	+	Glencree/Irland, Grave 2	Body washed ashore 26.10.1940
	Gefr	+	Glencree/Irland, Grave 1	Body washed ashore 26.10.1940
	Oblt	+	Cannock Chase/UK, Block 7, Row 8, Grave 190	Body washed ashore 07.11.1940

Date	Unit	Type	W/Nr	Codes	Name	Role
11.10.1940	2./Kü.Fl.Gr. 606	Do 17 Z-3	3475	7T+EK	Weber, Eugen	Bordmechaniker
11.10.1940	5./KG 2	Do 17 Z	2893	U5+AN	Bruske, Oskar	Bordschütze
11.10.1940	5./KG 2	Do 17 Z	2893	U5+AN	Fechner, Willi	Bordfunker
11.10.1940	5./KG 2	Do 17 Z	2893	U5+AN	Hubner, Johann	Flugzeugführer
11.10.1940	5./KG 2	Do 17 Z	2893	U5+AN	Schreiner, Georg	Bombenschütze
14.10.1940	2./NJG 2	Do 17 Z-10	2851	R4+DK	Dreher, Kurt	Bordschütze
14.10.1940	2./NJG 2	Do 17 Z-10	2851	R4+DK	Goetz, Erich	Flugzeugführer
14.10.1940	2./NJG 2	Do 17 Z-10	2851	R4+DK	Herden, Georg	Bordfunker
15.10.1940	3./KG 2	Do 17 Z			Brüdern, Hans-Joachim	Flugzeugführer
15.10.1940	3./KG 2	Do 17 Z			Fehrenbach, Heinrich	Bordfunker
15.10.1940	3./KG 2	Do 17 Z			Fellmann, Hans	Bordschütze
15.10.1940	3./KG 2	Do 17 Z			Trinkner, Richard	
16.10.1940	2./Kü.Fl.Gr. 606	Do 17 Z-3	2691	7T+HK	Blanck, Erwin	Beobachter
16.10.1940	2./Kü.Fl.Gr. 606	Do 17 Z-3	2691	7T+HK	Faupel, Heinrich	Flugzeugführer
16.10.1940	2./Kü.Fl.Gr. 606	Do 17 Z-3	2691	7T+HK	Schnake, Wilhelm	Bordmechaniker
16.10.1940	2./Kü.Fl.Gr. 606	Do 17 Z-3	2691	7T+HK	Steppat, Gerhard	Bordfunker
16.10.1940	3./Kü.Fl.Gr. 606	Do 17 Z-3	2682	7T+LL	Faehrmann, Rudolf	Bordfunker
16.10.1940	3./Kü.Fl.Gr. 606	Do 17 Z-3	2682	7T+LL	Havemann, Heinz	Beobachter
16.10.1940	3./Kü.Fl.Gr. 606	Do 17 Z-3	2682	7T+LL	Hölscher, Karl	Bordmechaniker
16.10.1940	3./Kü.Fl.Gr. 606	Do 17 Z-3	2682	7T+LL	Löcknitz, Gerhard	Flugzeugführer

DORNIER Do 17 CREW CASUALTIES

Exec	Rank	Fate	Burial	Notes
	Uffz	Missing		
	Flg	+	Bourdon/France, Block 6, Row 2, Grave 77	
	Ogefr	+	Bourdon/France, Block 19, Row 11, Grave 420	
	Lt	+	Bourdon/France, Block 6, Row 2, Grave 75	
	Gefr	+	Bourdon/France, Block 6, Row 2, Grave 66	
	Uffz	Wounded		
	Uffz	Wounded		
	Uffz	Wounded		
	Lt			
	Uffz			
	Gefr	PoW		
	Uffz			
	Oblt.z.S	+	Cannock Chase/UK, Block 6, Row 18, Grave 365	
	Fw	+	Cannock Chase/UK, Block 6, Row 18, Grave 363	
	Ogefr	+	Cannock Chase/UK, Block 6, Row 18, Grave 362	
	Fw	+	Cannock Chase/UK, Block 6, Row 18, Grave 364	
	Gefr	+	Cannock Chase/UK, Block 9, Row 1, Grave 2	
	Lt.z.S	+	Cannock Chase/UK, Block 9, Row 1, Grave 2	
	Uffz	+	Cannock Chase/UK, Block 9, Row 1, Grave 2	
	Uffz	+	Cannock Chase/UK, Block 9, Row 1, Grave 2	

Date	Unit	Type	W/Nr	Codes	Name	Role
16.10.1940	6./KG 2	Do 17 Z-3	3352	U5+CC	Patzke, Willi	Bordmechaniker
16.10.1940	1./KG 76	Do 17 Z-3	3448	F1+FH	Beer, Willi	Hilfsbeobachter
16.10.1940	1./KG 76	Do 17 Z-3	3448	F1+FH	Ott, Karl	Flugzeugführer
16.10.1940	1./KG 76	Do 17 Z-3	3448	F1+FH	Schneider, Georg	Bordmechaniker
16.10.1940	1./KG 76	Do 17 Z-3	3448	F1+FH	Schneidereit, Alfred	Bordfunker
17.10.1940	Stabsst./KG 2	Do 17 Z-2	3349	U5+EA	Hamann, Georg-Wilhelm	Beobachter
17.10.1940	Stabsst./KG 2	Do 17 Z-2	3349	U5+EA	Schöbel, Willi	Bordfunker
17.10.1940	Stabsst./KG 2	Do 17 Z-2	3349	U5+EA	Tilke, Wilhelm	Flugzeugführer
17.10.1940	Stabsst./KG 2	Do 17 Z-2	3349	U5+EA	Wörner, Georg	Bordschütze
18.10.1940	Stabsst./KG 2	Do 17 Z-3	2674		Brey, Heinrich	Beobachter
18.10.1940	Stabsst./KG 2	Do 17 Z-3	2674		Gravener, Herbert	Bordmechaniker
18.10.1940	Stabsst./KG 2	Do 17 Z-3	2674		Lintz, Friedrich	Bordfunker
18.10.1940	Stabsst./KG 2	Do 17 Z-3	2674		Steudel, Eberhard	Flugzeugführer
19.10.1940	8./KG 2	Do 17 Z-2	1153		Johannes, Albert	Bordschütze
19.10.1940	8./KG 2	Do 17 Z-2	3432		Köhler, Heinz	Bordmechaniker
19.10.1940	8./KG 2	Do 17 Z-2	3432		Steudel, Josef	Flugzeugführer
19.10.1940	8./KG 2	Do 17 Z-2	3432		Wachtel, Gotthardt	Bordfunker
19.10.1940	8./KG 2	Do 17 Z-2	3432		Waldmann, Otto	Hilfsbeobachter
21.10.1940	7./KG 76	Do 17 Z	3397	F1+LS	Blaschke, Kurt	Bordmechaniker
21.10.1940	7./KG 76	Do 17 Z	3397	F1+LS	Liesche, Fritz	Flugzeugführer
21.10.1940	7./KG 76	Do 17 Z	3397	F1+LS	Stößer, Georg	Bordfunker
21.10.1940	7./KG 76	Do 17 Z	3397	F1+LS	Wildhagen, Karl	Beobachter
22.10.1940	1./Kü.Fl.Gr. 606	Do 17 Z-5	2783	7T+AH	Küttner, Martin	Bordmechaniker
22.10.1940	1./Kü.Fl.Gr. 606	Do 17 Z-5	2783	7T+AH	Schörnich, Fritz	Bordfunker

DORNIER Do 17 CREW CASUALTIES

Exec	Rank	Fate	Burial	Notes
	Fw	Wounded		
	Uffz	+		
	Fw	+	Beauvais/France, Block 1, Row 2, Grave 63	
	Uffz	+	Beauvais/France, Block 1, Row 2, Grave 48	
	Ofw	+	Beauvais/France, Block 1, Row 2, Grave 53	
	Uffz	+	Bourdon/France, Block 6, Row 2, Grave 78	
	Obgfr	+	Bourdon/France, Block 6, Row 3, Grave 81	
	Ofw	+	Bourdon/France, Block 6, Row 2, Grave 79	
	Gefr	+	Bourdon/France, Block 6, Row 3, Grave 82	
	Fw	+	Düsseldorf-Nordfriedhof, Feld 111, Grave 840	
	Ogefr	+		
	Ogefr	+	Düsseldorf-Nordfriedhof, Feld 111, Grave 841	
	Lt	+	Erfurt-Hauptfriedhof	
	Uffz	+		
	Gefr			
	Lt	Wounded		
	Uffz	Wounded		
	Ofw	Wounded		
	Fw	Missing		
	Fw	Missing		
	Fw	+		Body washed ashore
	Lt	Missing		
	Uffz	PoW		
	Uffz	PoW		

Date	Unit	Type	W/Nr	Codes	Name	Role
22.10.1940	1./Kü.Fl.Gr. 606	Do 17 Z-5	2783	7T+AH	Stirnat, Walter	Flugzeugführer
22.10.1940	1./Kü.Fl.Gr. 606	Do 17 Z-5	2783	7T+AH	Würdemann, Heinrich	Beobachter
24.10.1940	1./KG 2	Do 17 Z	2598		Faust, Kurt	Bordschütze
24.10.1940	1./KG 2	Do 17 Z	2598		Meyer, Hans	Flugzeugführer
24.10.1940	1./KG 2	Do 17 Z	2598		Schmermaes, Wilhelm	Bordfunker
24.10.1940	1./KG 2	Do 17 Z	2598		Wolf, Wilhelm	Beobachter
24.10.1940	1./KG 2	Do 17 Z	3444		Dilger, Robert	Flugzeugführer
24.10.1940	1./KG 2	Do 17 Z	3444		Fürst, Helmuth	Bordfunker
24.10.1940	1./KG 2	Do 17 Z	3444		Kuntze, Karl	Bombenschütze
24.10.1940	1./KG 2	Do 17 Z	3444		Maaß, Karl	Bordschütze
24.10.1940	9./KG 2	Do 17 Z-2	2863		Bohnhof, Martin	Bordfunker
24.10.1940	9./KG 2	Do 17 Z-2	2863		Elbers, Wilhelm	Bordmechaniker
24.10.1940	9./KG 2	Do 17 Z-2	2863		Schinz, Günter	Beobachter
25.10.1940	4.(F)/14	Do 17 P	4158	5F+KM	Claus, Bernhard	Beobachter
25.10.1940	4.(F)/14	Do 17 P	4158	5F+KM	Höcker, Helmut	Flugzeugführer
25.10.1940	4.(F)/14	Do 17 P	4158	5F+KM	Mader, Rudi	Bordfunker
25.10.1940	8./KG 76	Do 17 Z	2882		Faller, Albert	Bordfunker
25.10.1940	8./KG 76	Do 17 Z	2882		Jöckel, Reinhard	Flugzeugführer
25.10.1940	8./KG 76	Do 17 Z	2882		Rumpel, Hermenegild	Bordmechaniker

DORNIER Do 17 CREW CASUALTIES

Exec	Rank	Fate	Burial	Notes
	Lt	PoW		
	Lt.z.S	PoW		
	Gefr	+	Bourdon/France, Block 22, Row 12, Grave 441	
	Uffz	+	Bourdon/France, Block 22, Row 12, Grave 438	
	Uffz	+	Bourdon/France, Block 22, Row 12, Grave 440	
	Ogefr	+	Bourdon/France, Block 22, Row 12, Grave 439	
	Fw	+	Bourdon/France, Block 22, Row 12, Grave 434	
	Ogefr	+	Bourdon/France, Block 22, Row 12, Grave 436	
	Ogefr	+	Bourdon/France, Block 22, Row 12, Grave 435	
	Gefr	+	Bourdon/France, Block 22, Row 12, Grave 437	
	Fw	Wounded		
	Gefr	Wounded/ +	Lowestoft (Beccles Road) Cemetery, Suffolk/UK, Block 24, Grave 512	
	Gefr	+	Bourdon/France, Block 22, Row 12, Grave 442	
	Uffz	+		
	Lt	+	La Cambe/Frankreich, Block 36, Grave 114	
	Uffz	+	La Cambe/Frankreich, Block 36, Grave 115	
	Ofw	+		
	Ofw	+	Champigny-St.Andre/France, Block 17, Grave 279	
	Fw	+		

DORNIER Do 17 IN THE BATTLE OF BRITAIN

Date	Unit	Type	W/Nr	Codes	Name	Role
25.10.1940	8./KG 76	Do 17 Z	2882		Sachs, Ewald	Hilfsbeobachter
27.10.1940	3./KG 2	Do 17 Z-2	3443	U5+HL	Broich, Peter	Flugzeugführer
27.10.1940	3./KG 2	Do 17 Z-2	3443	U5+HL	Heimann, Helmut	Bordfunker
27.10.1940	3./KG 2	Do 17 Z-2	3443	U5+HL	Krempel, Karl-Heinz	Beobachter
27.10.1940	3./KG 2	Do 17 Z-2	3443	U5+HL	Ruttkowski, Hans	Bordmechaniker
27.10.1940	7./KG 3	Do 17 Z			Päßler, Horst	Bombenschütze
27.10.1940	9./KG 3	Do 17 Z			Heese, Karl	Bordfunker
27.10.1940	7./KG 76	Do 17 Z-2	1150	F1+HR	Carl, Richard	Bordfunker
27.10.1940	7./KG 76	Do 17 Z-2	1150	F1+HR	Ebeling, Friedhelm	Flugzeugführer
27.10.1940	7./KG 76	Do 17 Z-2	1150	F1+HR	Fritz, Karl	Bombenschütze
27.10.1940	7./KG 76	Do 17 Z-2	1150	F1+HR	Johannes, Erich	Bordmechaniker
27.10.1940	7./KG 76	Do 17 Z-2	1150	F1+HR	Wülpern, Gustav	Bordschütze
28.10.1940	1./KG 3	Do 17 Z-2	2544	5K+CH	Hausdorf, Harald	Bordmechaniker
28.10.1940	1./KG 3	Do 17 Z-2	2544	5K+CH	Nitzsch, Rudi	Bordfunker
28.10.1940	1./KG 3	Do 17 Z-2	2544	5K+CH	Schreiber, Albin	Hilfsbeobachter
28.10.1940	1./KG 3	Do 17 Z-2	2544	5K+CH	Voßhage, Kurt	Flugzeugführer
28.10.1940	8./KG 3	Do 17 Z			Büttner, Walter	Bordschütze
28.10.1940	8./KG 3	Do 17 Z			Ziepusch, Josef	Bordfunker
30.10.1940	3.(F)/10	Do 17 P			Baucks, Ernst	Flugzeugführer

DORNIER Do 17 CREW CASUALTIES

Exec	Rank	Fate	Burial	Notes
	Fw	+	Champigny-St.Andre/France, Block 17, Grave 275	
	Fw			
	Uffz			
	Oblt			
	Uffz	Wounded		
	Fw	+	Lommel/Belgium, Block 21, Grave 216	
	Fw	Wounded		
	Uffz	+	Cannock Chase/UK, Block 1, Row 8, Grave 311	Body washed ashore 30.03.1941
	Uffz	+	Cannock Chase/UK, Block 1, Row 8, Grave 312	
	Uffz	+	Felixstowe New cemetery, Suffolk/UK, Block K/B, Grave 6	Body washed ashore 15.12.1940
	Uffz	Missing		
	Ogefr	+	Cannock Chase/UK, Block 1, Row 6, Grave 227	Body washed ashore 11.12.1940
	Uffz	+	Cannock Chase/UK, Block 5, Row 1, Grave 3	
	Fw	+	Cannock Chase/UK, Block 5, Row 1, Grave 4	
	Fw	PoW/+	Maidstone Cemetery, Kent/ UK, Block CC, Row 1, Grave 284	
	Fw	PoW		
	Gefr	Wounded		
	Flg	Wounded		
	Ofw	Wounded		

APPENDICES

Appendix I

Main Dornier Do 17 Combat Variants in the Battle of Britain

Do 17 M-1 (recce)	Bramo Fafnir 323 A-1 engines. 3 x 7.92mm machine-guns up to 1,000kg bomb load. Originally designed as a bomber, was used in the reconnaissance role in the Battle of Britain.
Do 17 P-1 (recce)	BMW 132N. 3 x 7.92mm machine-guns, 2 x cameras and photo flash bombs.
Do 17 P-2 (recce)	BMW 132N. As P-1 but up to 200kg bomb load.
Do 17 Z-1	Bramo Fafnir 323 A-1 engines. 4 x 7.92mm machine-guns, up to 500kg bomb load.
Do 17 Z-2	Bramo Fafnir 323 P. As Z-1 up to 6 x 7.92mm machine-guns up to 1,000kg bomb load.
Do 17 Z-3	Bramo Fafnir 323 P. As Z-2 but reduced bomb load and additional automatic cameras.
Do 17 Z-5	Bramo Fafnir 323 P. As Z-3 but additional flotation aids on nose and internal life-saving equipment.
Do 17 Z-7 (night fighter)	Bramo Fafnir 323 P. Offensive armament of 3 x 7.92mm machine-guns and 1 x 20mm cannon. Known as *Kauz* I.
Do 17 Z-10 (night fighter)	Bramo Fafnir 323 P. As Z-7 4 x 7.92mm machine-guns, 2 x 20mm cannon, infra-red spotlight. 6 x boxes of 15 x 1kg incendiaries to be manually dropped. Known as *Kauz* II.

Appendix II

Dornier Do 17 Combat Units on 13 August 1940

Unit	Type	Base	Commanding Officer
Westa 1/ObdL	Do 17 Z	Oldenburg	Oberleutnant Kurt Jonas
2.(F)/11	Do 17 P	Bernay	Major Richard Paulitsch
4.(F)/14	Do 17 M/P/Bf 110	Cherbourg	Hauptmann Franz Kusatz
Aufkl (F)/22	Do 17 P	Trondheim	Oberstleutnant Erik Thomas
3.(F)/31	Do 17 P	St Brieuc	Hauptmann Johannes Sieckenius
1.(F)/120	Do 17 P	Stavanger	Major Anton Schub
4.(F)/121	Do 17 P	Villacoublay	Hauptmann Ulrich Kerber
5.(F)/122	Do 17 P	Haute-Fontaine	Hauptmann Herbert Böhm
2.(F)/123	Do 17 P	Cherbourg	Hauptmann Günter Hurlin
Westa 26	Do 17 Z	Grimbergen	Hauptmann Sigmund Frhr von Rottberg
Westa 51	Do 17	Buc	Oberleutnant Kurt Kreowski
KG 2	Do 17 Z	St Leger	Oberst Johannes Fink
I./KG 2	Do 17 Z	Epinoy	Major Martin Gutzmann
II./KG 2	Do 17 Z	St Leger	Oberstleutnant Paul Weitkus
III./KG 2	Do 17 Z	Cambrai-Sud	Major Adolf Fuchs
KG 3	Do 17 Z	Le Culot	Oberst Wolfgang Chamier-Glisczinski
I./KG 3	Do 17 Z	Le Culot	Oberstleutnant Rudolf Gabelmann/ Oberst Karl Frhr von Wechmar
II./KG 3	Do 17 Z	Antwerp-Deurne	Hauptmann Otto Pilger
III./KG 3	Do 17 Z	St Trond	Hauptmann Erich Rathmann
KG 76	Do 17 Z	Cormeilles	Oberstleutnant Stefan Fröhlich
I./KG 76	Do 17 Z	Beauvais	Major Ludwig Schulz

DORNIER Do 17 IN THE BATTLE OF BRITAIN

Unit	Type	Base	Commanding Officer
III./KG 76	Do 17 Z	Cormeilles	Major Alois Lindmayr
II./NJG 1	Do 17 Z	Düsseldorf	Hauptmann Karl-Heinrich Heyse
Stab./StG 1	Do 17 M	Angers	Major Walter Hagen
Stab./StG 2	Do 17 M	St Malo	Major Oskar Dinort
Stab./StG 3	Do 17 M/Z	Bretigny	Oberst Karl Angerstein
Stab./StG 77	Do 17 M	Caen	Hauptmann Clemens von Schönborn-Wiesentheid
Kü.Fl.Gr 606	Do 17 Z	Hahn	Oberstleutnant Joachim Hahn

Appendix III

Other Battle of Britain Dornier Do 17 Units

Aufkl.(F) 10	Do 17 P	Various	
Auflk. (F) 21	Do 17 P	Bergen-op-Zoom	Major Konrad Graf von Uxkül-Gyllenband
Aufkl. (F)121	Do 17		Various

Appendix IV

Major Executive Officers in Dornier Do 17 Offensive Units

10 July – 31 October 1940

KG 2

Komm	Oberst Johannes Fink	Until 20 October 1940
	Oberst Herbert Rieckhoff	
I Gruppe	Major Martin Gutzmann	PoW 26 August 1940
	Major Waldemar Lerche	
1 Staffel	Oberleutnant Karl Kessel	Until 19 September 1940
	Hauptmann Hans-Uwe Ortmann	
2 Staffel	Oberleutnant Helmut Powolny	
3 Staffel	Hauptmann Walter Krieger	PoW 10 July 1940
	Oberleutnant Gottfried Buchholz	
II Gruppe	Oberstleutnant Paul Weitkus	Until December 1940
4 Staffel	Oberleutnant Joachim Genzow	
5 Staffel	Hauptmann Erich Machetzki	+ 12 July 1940
	Hauptmann Ulrich Linnemann	
6 Staffel	Oberleutnant Gerhard Czernik	
III Gruppe	Major Adolf Fuchs	Wounded 31 August 1940
	Major Klaus Uebe	Until 20 March 1941
7 Staffel	Oberleutnant Gerhard Schrödter	Until February 1941
8 Staffel	Oberleutnant Friedrich Wilhelm von Stieglitz	Until 15 July 1940
	Oberleutnant Werner Morich	+ 13 August 1940
	Hauptmann Hubertus Lessmann	Wounded 15 September 1940
	Hauptmann Martin Kästner	
9 Staffel	Oberleutnant Bruno Davids	Until September 1940
	Hauptmann Walter Bradel	

MAJOR EXECUTIVE OFFICERS IN DORNIER Do 17 OFFENSIVE UNITS

KG 3

Komm	Oberst Wolfgang von Chamier Glisczisnki	
I Gruppe	Oberst Rudolf Gabelmann	Until July 1940
	Major Wilhelm Georg Kunowski	August 1940
	Oberst Karl Frhr von Wechmar	
1 Staffel	Oberleutnant Rudolf Graf von Platen-Hallermund (?)	+ 29 August 1940
2 Staffel	Oberleutnant Otto Köhnke	Wounded 15 August 1940
	Oberleutnant Werner Lemme (?)	
3 Staffel	Hauptmann Rolf Kückens	+ 8 September 1940
	Oberleutnant Ernst Wilhelm Ihrig (Hauptmann Günther Dörfel, 3./KG 3, October 1940?)	
II Gruppe	Hauptmann Otto Pilger	
4 Staffel	Oberleutnant Bernhard Granicky	
5 Staffel	Hauptmann Ernst Puttmann	+ 15 September 1940
	Oberleutnant Rudolf Guhl (?)	
6 Staffel	Oberleutnant Herbert Schwartz	PoW 21 August 1940
	Oberleutnant Peter-Paul Breu	
III Gruppe	Major Erich Rathmann	
7 Staffel	Oberleutnant Siegfried Jungklaus (?)	
8 Staffel	*Unidentified*	
9 Staffel	Oberleutnant Joachim Jödicke	From July 1940

KG 76

Komm	Oberstleutnant Stefan Fröhlich	
I Gruppe	Major Theodore Schweitzer	
	Hauptmann Robert von Sichart	
1 Staffel	Oberleutnant Hanns Heise	
2 Staffel	Oberleutnant Rolf Hallensleben	
3 Staffel	Hauptmann Eberhard Wöhlermann	
III Gruppe	Oberstleutnant Adolf Genth	+ 29 July 1940
	Major Alois Lindmayr	From 5 August 1940
7 Staffel	*Unidentified*	
8 Staffel	Oberleutnant Heinrich Schweickardt	
9 Staffel	Hauptmann Joachim Roth	PoW 18 August 1940

KG 77

(Converted to the Junkers Ju 88 in July 1940)

Komm	General major Heinz-Hellmuth von Wühlisch
I Gruppe	Major Rolf Balcke
1 Staffel	Major Theodor Schweitzer
2 Staffel	Major Werner Leutchenberg
3 Staffel	Hauptmann Paul-Friedrich Darjes
II Gruppe	Major Franz Behrendt
4 Staffel	Oberleutnant Hans-Georg Leuze (?)
5 Staffel	Hauptmann Wilhelm Bues
6 Staffel	Oberleutnant Ernst Berbecker
III Gruppe	Major Max Kless
7 Staffel	Oberleutnant Fritz Uhl
8 Staffel	Oberleutnant Dieter Pfeiffer
9 Staffel	Hauptmann Jakob Neuen

Küstenfliegergruppe 606

Kdr	Oberstleutnant Hermann Edert	Until 27 July 1940
	Major Joachim Hahn	
1 Staffel	Hauptmann Wolfgang Lenschow	
2 Staffel	Hauptmann Werner Lassmann	Until January 1941
3 Staffel	Hauptmann Heinrich Golcher	

5./NJG 1

(From June 1940; Became 2./NJG 2 in September 1940. Flew mainly Ju 88 C-2/C-4)

Kdr	Major Karl Heyse	+ 23 November 1940
St Kap	Hauptmann Rolf Jung	

Bibliography

Balke, Ulf *Der Luftkrieg in Europa 1939-1941* (Bernard & Graefe Verlag, 1989)

Foreman, John *RAF Fighter Command Victory Claims of World War 2. Part 1 1939-1940* (Red Kite, 2003)

Goss, Chris, *Dornier 17 in Focus* (Red Kite, 2005)

_____, *Dornier Do 17: The Luftwaffe's Flying Pencil* (Frontline, 2018)

_____, *Dornier Do 17 Combat Units of World War 2* (Osprey, 2019)

_____, *Dornier Do 17: The Flying Pencil in Luftwaffe Service* (Crecy, 2020)

Parker, Nigel, *Luftwaffe Crash Archive Volumes 1-6* (Red Kite, 2013-2014)

Parry, Simon, W *Battle of Britain Combat Archive Volumes 1-8 (*Red Kite, 2016-2020)

Ramsey, Winston (Ed.), *The Blitz Then and Now Vols 1 & 2* (After the Battle, 1987, 1988)

Acknowledgements

This is my fifth (and probably final) book in one form or another on the ubiquitous Dornier Do 17 – nicknamed the Flying Pencil on account of its slender fuselage.

When Martin Mace of Pen and Sword suggested a photograph-based publication on the Do 17 purely covering the Battle of Britain, I did baulk. However, since the publication of *Dornier Do 17: The Flying Pencil in Luftwaffe Service* (Crecy, Manchester, 2020), new photographs have continued to emerge, so this suggestion gave me the opportunity to concentrate purely on combat losses or losses by operational units during the period July to October 1940.

This time, I have been given a boost by Matti Salonen's database of both Do 17 aircraft losses and personnel casualties which for the first time, thanks to Matti's generous agreement and with additional research by myself, will give the reader the definitive story of the Do 17 in respect of photographs and losses during the Battle of Britain.

In addition, I would like to thank Tim Oliver, Andy Saunders, Peter Cornwell and the late Dr Alfred Price for their help over the years, not to mention Bernd Rauchbach for his advice, corrections and proof reading. Also, my thanks go to relatives of Do 17 pilots; Barbara, George and John Wolff in Canada and the USA; and the late Günther Steudel in Canada.

Günther passed away suddenly and unexpectedly early in 2022, and, therefore, I would like to dedicate this book to him and his father, Joseph 'Sepp' Steudel, who flew the Do 17 with III./KG 2 from 1940 to 1944.